D0329162

SECOND EDITION

# *Promoting* YOUR ACTING CAREER

*A Step-by-Step Guide to Opening the Right Doors*

GLENN ALTERMAN

**ALLWORTH PRESS**
NEW YORK

*This book is dedicated to*
*my former acting teachers:*

Harold Guskin
Wynn Handman
Michael Howard
Terry Schreiber
Larry Moss
Mira Rostova
Michael Moriarty

©1998, 2004 Glenn Alterman

Published by Allworth Press
An imprint of Allworth Communications
10 East 23rd Street, New York, NY 10010

Cover design by Derek Bacchus

Interior design by Sharp Des!gns, Holt, MI

Page composition/typography by Integra Software Services, Pvt. Ltd., Pondicherry, India

ISBN: 1-58115-391-0

Library of Congress Cataloging-in-Publication Data

Alterman, Glenn, 1946-
  Promoting your acting career: a step-by-step guide to opening the right doors/Glenn Alterman.—2nd ed.
    p. cm.
  Includes index.
  ISBN: 1-58115-391-0 (pbk.)
  1. Acting—Vocational guidance. I. Title.

PN2055.A455 2004
792.02'8'023—dc22                    2004020012

Printed in Canada

# *Contents*

Acknowledgments . . . . . . . . . . . . . . . . . . . . . . . . . . . . . . .   v

Preface  . . . . . . . . . . . . . . . . . . . . . . . . . . . . . . . . . . . .   vii

1. Actor Training . . . . . . . . . . . . . . . . . . . . . . . . . . . . . .   1

2. Headshots: Your Calling Card . . . . . . . . . . . . . . . . . . . . .   17

3. Now That the Photo Session Is Over,
   What Next? . . . . . . . . . . . . . . . . . . . . . . . . . . . . . . . . .   25

4. Interviews with Photographers and Reproduction
   Studio Owners  . . . . . . . . . . . . . . . . . . . . . . . . . . . . . .   31

5. Resumes . . . . . . . . . . . . . . . . . . . . . . . . . . . . . . . . . .   41

6. Mailing Campaigns and Promotional Marketing . . . . . . . .   51

7. Personal Marketing . . . . . . . . . . . . . . . . . . . . . . . . . . .   59

8. Getting and Preparing for Interviews and Auditions . . . . .   65

9. Videotapes  . . . . . . . . . . . . . . . . . . . . . . . . . . . . . . . .   73

10.  Interviews with Videographers and Video Editors . . . . . . .  79

11.  Actor Directories . . . . . . . . . . . . . . . . . . . . . . . . . . . . . . . .  85

12.  Promoting Your Career on the Internet . . . . . . . . . . . . . . .  89

13.  Networking . . . . . . . . . . . . . . . . . . . . . . . . . . . . . . . . . . . .  93

14.  Networking Facilities . . . . . . . . . . . . . . . . . . . . . . . . . . . .  101

15.  Talent Tours . . . . . . . . . . . . . . . . . . . . . . . . . . . . . . . . . . .  107

16.  Talent Agents . . . . . . . . . . . . . . . . . . . . . . . . . . . . . . . . . .  111

17.  Interviews with Talent Agents . . . . . . . . . . . . . . . . . . . . .  115

18.  Personal Managers . . . . . . . . . . . . . . . . . . . . . . . . . . . . . .  127

19.  Interviews with Personal Managers . . . . . . . . . . . . . . . . .  129

20.  Casting Directors . . . . . . . . . . . . . . . . . . . . . . . . . . . . . . .  137

21.  Publicists . . . . . . . . . . . . . . . . . . . . . . . . . . . . . . . . . . . . .  167

22.  Voice-overs . . . . . . . . . . . . . . . . . . . . . . . . . . . . . . . . . . . .  173

23.  Interviews with Voice-over Specialists . . . . . . . . . . . . . . .  179

24.  Working on Daytime Serials . . . . . . . . . . . . . . . . . . . . . . .  187

25.  Producing Your Own Play . . . . . . . . . . . . . . . . . . . . . . . . .  189

26.  The One-Person Show . . . . . . . . . . . . . . . . . . . . . . . . . . . .  197

27.  Independent Films . . . . . . . . . . . . . . . . . . . . . . . . . . . . . .  205

28.  Creating Your Own Theater Company . . . . . . . . . . . . . . .  215

29.  Artists' Support Organizations, Career Consultants,
     and Life, Career, and Creativity Coaches . . . . . . . . . . . . .  223


     Appendix: New York Theaters . . . . . . . . . . . . . . . . . . . .  229

     About the Author . . . . . . . . . . . . . . . . . . . . . . . . . . . . . . .  236

     Index . . . . . . . . . . . . . . . . . . . . . . . . . . . . . . . . . . . . . . . .  239

# Acknowledgments

I wish to thank the following people for their help with this book: Andre DeShields, Bunny Levine, David Zema, Barry Hoff, Eva Charney, Doug Barron, Carlotta Bogavianos, Linda Chapman (New York Theatre Workshop), Merle Frimark, Herbert Rubens, Spider Duncan Christopher, Michael Warren Powell, Lee K. Bohlen, Karen Kayser, Alan Nusbaum, Joe Stern (the Matrix Theatre), Martin Gage, Jonn Wasser, Shirley Rich—and all of the photographers, casting directors, artistic directors of theater companies, publicists, reproduction studio owners, videographers, actors, and many others who granted interviews, took my phone calls, and provided the invaluable information that aided in the writing of this book.

Thank you all very much.

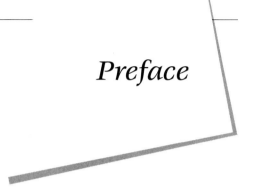

# *Preface*

**Promote** 1. to advance in station, rank, or honor 2. to contribute to the growth or prosperity of; further 3. to help bring into being; launch

I decided to write this book after noticing that many of my actor friends, although very talented, were constantly unemployed. I knew for a fact that they were out there pushing to get work, but success eluded many of them. There is a belief that if you have talent, study, go to every audition, send pictures and resumes, and pursue your dream with fervor, you'll make it. And there's another notion that if you're really talented, someone will somehow "discover" you. This book was written out of the realization that these beliefs aren't completely true. Show business is a business. And like any business, it must be approached with a strategy, a game plan, and the proper artillery. There are specific ways to achieve what you dream about. This book was written for the actor who is ready and willing to work.

The first place that most casting directors and talent agents look on an actor's resume is training. It all begins with how well trained you are. Most actors begin their careers with a great deal of passion and a desire to succeed. But learning your craft and honing your skills are important contributing factors to how well you will succeed in your career. For that reason, the first chapter of this book deals with (in depth) the all-important subject of actor training.

Headshots are one of the main promotional tools available to an actor. But before you even think of calling a photographer, you must have a firm understanding of what specific "type" you are and must know specifically how you plan on marketing yourself. In the book, I discuss understanding what type you are and the best ways to market yourself. Without a thorough understanding of marketing, there's a good chance that your headshot, although personally flattering, might not be totally effective.

While researching this book, I learned that there's more to a mailing campaign than just sending out headshots and postcards. Actors must be very specific as to who they target, why, and how. Initial cover letters must be well thought out. Remember, this is the first impression casting directors and agents will have of you. Follow-up mailings must be thorough and well planned. I suggest effective ways to make every mailing count. The idea is to get your readers' attention and interest immediately.

Throughout the book, I look at the many ways actors can promote themselves, from making videotapes or voice-over demos to producing one-person shows or independent films. I think you'll discover as you go through the book that there's a great deal you can do for yourself besides sitting home and waiting for that phone to ring.

I believe that you'll find the chapter on networking to be an eye-opener. While researching this subject, I realized that I never really knew the first thing about effective networking. One lesson I learned is that it's a lot more than a friendly hello and handshake at a party. It's one of the major ways that the business is run. If you walk away from this book with nothing but a thorough understanding of how to effectively network in show business, I think you'll have achieved a great deal.

Although I interviewed over one hundred people for the book, I included only the most informative interviews. Agents, casting directors, managers, photographers, voice-over specialists, videographers, and more are all represented. I asked questions that I felt every actor would want answered. The section on casting directors is by far the largest one in the book. I was very fortunate to get interviews with some of the most powerful casting directors in the business. I am extremely grateful for their willingness to share what I feel is invaluable information. You'll find the answers to such questions as—What do you look for at an audition (and interview)? What is the one thing that really ticks you off about actors? If you had one piece of advice to offer actors about their careers, what would it be?— particularly illuminating. I know I did.

The task of getting casting directors, agents, producers, and directors to know who you are is not easy. Turning a talented, struggling actor into a steadily working one can be accomplished with perseverance, tact, and know-how. That's what this book is about. It's written for the actor who just got off the bus as well as for the seasoned professional.

In this updated edition, I've made significant revisions. Security changes since 9/11 have altered some of the ways actors must now seek employment. This new edition includes a great deal of information not included in the last. You'll notice several new chapters in this revision.

For example, I've included a chapter on finding work in daytime serials. There are many misconceptions about the work on soaps and the types of actors that are hired. I've tried to debunk some of these misconceptions.

The Internet is quickly becoming a major source for of information for casting and upcoming productions. I've listed many of the most important Web sites.

The book also includes information on career and life consultants, a listing of the most active theaters in the New York City area, as well as many new and exciting interviews.

I feel that this revised edition has the most up-to-date information about the business. I hope you'll find it helpful and a good reference book when you have any questions regarding your own career.

Seeking a career in show business can be a difficult undertaking. I've written this guide to make the journey a bit less perilous. I sincerely wish you the best of luck in your attempts to meet your goals and realize all of your dreams.

GLENN ALTERMAN

# Actor Training

**B**efore you begin marketing yourself as an actor, you should be certain that you're well trained and ready to start work. I can't tell you how often I have heard stories of actors who jumped the gun and started auditioning before they were actually ready. This can be damaging to a career down the road. Remember, every time you audition before a casting director, you're making an impression. If you're not ready yet, you may ruin your chances with that casting director for years to come. Don't go out there until you're certain you're ready. Actors need to constantly study to improve their craft. Just as an electrician or plumber must learn his trade, so should an actor. This is a profession. You must develop a technique that you can depend on, a way to approach the work. The more diversified your training, the more adept you'll be. I believe all actors develop their own way of working, based on their own sense of truth, the teachers they've studied with, and on-the-job training.

The acting class is the place to address your specific acting problems and emotional blocks. It's a place to stretch, overcome fears, try out roles that you might be right for. Most good acting schools create a supportive environment. Leave any acting class where the teacher is in any way abusive. Always trust your instincts if you feel uncomfortable with a teacher. Make sure that you are given enough classroom time to work. Remember, this is a performance art. I've seen classes where actors only get to do one scene a month. That's not enough classroom time.

Just because a teacher is one of the "name" teachers does not mean he is the best teacher for you. You must believe that what he's teaching is accurate and truthful. If you think he's full of it, leave.

### Selecting the Right Acting School for You

Here are some of the best ways to find the right acting teacher.

- Referrals are one of the best ways to find an acting school. Ask around. Network. Ask other actors whom they've studied with.
- What well-known actors have studied in this school, with this teacher? Most acting teachers are proud to list former students who have gone on to successful careers.
- See if you can audit a class before deciding to commit to a school.
- Where is the school or teacher located? Will you feel safe if you have to take class at night there?
- Would you want this school or teacher listed on your resume?
- How many students are in each class?
- How often will you get to work in the class?
- How expensive is the class? Are there work-study programs?
- Learn about the technique that is being taught at the school or by the teacher. Is it mainstream training such as Meisner or the Method, a compilation of methods, or is it something more avant-garde?
- What is the teacher's background? Where was he trained? What has he done professionally?
- Does this school offer scene nights or productions of its students' work for the public (casting directors, talent agents) to see?
- Will you be able to interview or audition for the teacher?
- How are the classes divided? How will it be decided what level you will be placed in?

- Are there make-up classes if you're out for work or illness, or do you lose your money for those classes?
- Does the Better Business Bureau have any complaints about this teacher or the school?

## Interviews with Acting Teachers

Here are some interviews with well-known acting teachers in the New York area.

SANDE SHURIN (**SS**) is the creator of the acting technique "Transformational Acting." She and her husband, playwright/talent agent Bruce Levy, founded the Sande Shurin Acting Studio in Manhattan in 1980. Her intensives and specialty workshops, such as "Camera Technique," are given at her two home-base acting studios as well as well as throughout the United States, Canada, and Europe. Ms. Shurin also privately coaches for film, TV, and theater. She has directed on Broadway and Off-Broadway, as well as directing the cable series "Working Actors."

SALLY JOHNSON (**SJ**), founder of The Sally Johnson Studio in NYC, has trained actors in the art of film acting for the past twenty-five years. Sally studied with Sanford Meisner, Lee Strasberg, and Charles Conrad. While enjoying a successful career herself, she opened the Sally Johnson Studio, which is now among the most respected and successful film acting studios in NYC. She has trained hundreds of actors who are working today.

GENE FRANKEL (**GF**) is a three-time OBIE Award winner for Best Director. He has also been awarded the Vernon Rice Award for Best Production and Direction, the first Lola D'Annunzio Award, and Playboy's Golden Owl Award. He was recognized by the Ford Foundation for distinguished service to the theater, and participated in the Cultural Exchange program for the U.S. Department by lecturing in Poland, Yugoslavia, and Russia. He has served as visiting professor at Columbia University, Boston College, New York University, and Queens College. His students have included Loretta Swit, Judd Hirsch, Marybeth Hurt, JoBeth Williams, Lee Marvin, James Coco, Rod Steiger, Dennis Weaver, and Morgan Freeman, among many others.

Penny Templeton (**PT**) began performing and studying under such masters as Paul Sorvino and Wynn Handman. Her unique coaching methods and techniques have garnered attention and recognition from industry peers. She has been called upon to offer her expertise for articles in national magazines. Ms. Templeton is a member of the Blue Ribbon Panel for the final judging of the Daytime Emmy Awards and has also been a finalist judge for the Cable Ace Awards and the New York Film Festival. In addition, she teaches "Acting for the Camera" to the third-year students in the Master's program at Columbia University.

---

### What specifically do you look for when you interview/audition actors?

**SS**: I look for their "essence"—what makes them special—and their willingness to take risks. I am not interested in how the actor says the words. I want to be engaged by their presence, the life they create, and their behavior. I want to have an experience of what's going on for them rather than what they want to show me. Spontaneity and creativity, along with that "essence," is what I look for.

**SJ**: I look for people who are excited about their craft. It's also important that they are aware of the commitment that acting requires and are responsible. If they are nervous when we first meet, that is fine; truth and vulnerability are compelling to me. I like them to be who they are. I look for someone who is willing to take risks.

**GF**: Everyone auditions for my classes. I give the actors certain exercises to do, which tells me a lot about them. One thing I look for is courage. Courage, to me, is more important than talent. Everyone has some talent, but courage is far more important. You need to go to those dark places where your talent tells you that you need to go. I look for talent, of course, but more important is the courage to explore.

**PT**: We are looking for actors who are brave, dedicated, and open. Actors who want to dig in and do the really hard work necessary to find the true artist in themselves.

**Is there a certain emphasis or technique that you use in your classes?**

**SS**: Transformational Acting starts with learning to open and use what I call "the emotional body," rather than relying on sense memory or any predetermined planning of what the actor is supposed to feel. The emotional body contains the actor's entire emotional range. Once you have accessed this emotional body and are living in the circumstances of the script, there is very little planning. The actor lives as the character and discovers with each take or performance the current truth of the moment. This technique is based on "self": what the actor is "really" currently feeling combined with being present to his uniqueness (star power). It is here that we learn to transform who we are into character. This allows the actor to "work in the moment" and make bold choices while illuminating the material.

**SJ**: My classes are for acting in film and television. The emphasis is on cold readings, auditions, and working in front of the camera. Trusting your instincts is essential. Listening and concentrating your attention on your partner, reading well off the page, emotional availability, and taking action on your impulses are all done with little or no rehearsal. Camerawork, including ECUs, close-ups, two-shots, and mastershots, is taught.

**GF**: The bottom line on everything I do is truth and insightful behavior. I teach my students to develop their instrument, develop the receptivity, the sensitivity, and the kind of energy and imagination they need. I use exercises to develop the instrument. Harold Clurman and Lee Strasberg were my greatest influences.

Then I work with students in scene study. Scene study involves finding the character's logical truth. To put it briefly, not everybody reacts to the same event in the same way. Conditioned by circumstances as well as background, people and characters react differently to different events. To me, the ultimate technique is trust. To develop the trust, you must have a technique to know what to trust. You must learn to be credible to yourself in order to be credible to other people: the audience, your fellow actors.

**PT**: The Penny Templeton Approach to Acting is grounded in the tra-
ditions of Stanislavski, the Method, and Meisner, with added new
techniques to empower the actors with training that will ease their
transition from acting class into the real world.

### Can you describe the format of your classes?

**SS**: Actors begin with an initial two-day advanced intensive or
a nine-week intermediate/beginner course, each providing the
actor with the same fundamental understanding of Transformational Acting. They then continue on to our ongoing classes, where
each class teaches a new or deeper understanding of a distinction
(aspect) of this technique. They then apply what they have learned
to a scene. Every actor works during the class and is given very
personal attention.

**SJ**: There are morning, afternoon, and evening classes offered. Each
class runs four hours and meets once a week. We open with a medita-
tion, relaxation, exercise, or a variety of other warm-ups. Next you have
a memorized or a cold-read scene to do on camera. Two cameras are
used to shoot the scene, and each student then has an edited copy of
his work to take home. There are twelve to twenty students per class,
and all classes are ongoing. An interview is required.

**GF**: We begin with warm-up exercises, first on the instrument. In the
more advanced classes we do scene study. We do scene analysis,
break up the scene into beats. But most important of all, we develop
a taste and feel for the event or events. It's not enough that the actor
gets an emotional surge. I never allow more than eighteen in a class.
In the summer we have a whole summer program.

**PT**: Penny's Technique Classes are a unique blend of exercises and
scene work. Every class begins with each actor getting up individually
for Penny's "Acting Barre," a five-part exercise that works all aspects of
the technique, including emotional and improvisation work. This is
followed by an on-camera exercise that changes month to month. This
second exercise works on a specific skill the actor should master, i.e.,

sensory work or cold auditions. The last part of the class is scene study. Every actor in class gets up for all three parts.

Penny's Advanced On-Camera Class is geared toward preparing the actors to deal with the rigorous demands of television and film. In addition to teaching the actors how to share their work with camera to get the most out of a scene they are also taught how to cope with the "on-set demands." The actors get a new scene each week. They do not know who their scene partner will be and there is no rehearsal. While the class does acting exercises with Penny in her studio, a "cast" is called to the "set," where their scene is blocked for multiple cameras. Their dress rehearsal is viewed by the class via closed-circuit. Notes are given and the scene is taped. All the work is played back on a ten-foot movie screen at the end of class for critique.

**Any advice that you have for actors pursuing an acting career?**

**SS**: Work! Work! Work! Stay in action and follow your dreams. Create your own opportunities, create your own material, but just keep working. It is in the process of work that the actor matures, develops, and meets people. Stay inspired and inspire those around you. And keep studying. You must constantly hone those skills. As you personally change and transform, so must your work. Find a school or teacher that supports your goals and dreams and one that you resonate with. Find a place that is safe for you to experiment and discover.

**SJ**: Commit fully to what you love. Your career depends on this combination of commitment and passion. This professional attitude will pull you through those times when nothing is happening in your career. Then, when your time does come, you'll be ready. Don't give up. Find people you respect and love to work with. Create your own work.

**GF**: First of all, find a place to stay. It's so disheartening. Make friends. Do background studies on the Internet. Speak to people who have been there. Network. Make sure this is what you want to do. I don't suggest going to Hollywood at first. It's very hard to start out there. It's hard to make friends there.

**PT**: Most actors want to rush out and start auditioning before they are really ready. The first impression you make on a casting director or agent will stay with them your entire career. With increasing speed and changes in the demands on the modern actor, many seek quick fixes that they hope will get them immediate work and launch their careers to stardom. Many have never taken a serious, in-depth acting class. They spend their time and money and energy on short-term specialty classes, which more often then not lead to patchy and incomplete training. It's unfortunate that so many discover the need for serious training only after spending all their money on these "fast-food" classes, which make big promises but leave them empty. Broke and disheartened, the "prodigal actor" finally realizes he has no technique. Real success is your personal growth as an actor. Be patient and master your craft.

### Acting Schools

What follows are some of the better-known acting schools in New York City. New York is certainly not the only place to get good acting training, but it is a well-known fact that many of the best teachers and schools are in New York.

The Acting Studio, Inc.
244 West 54th Street, 12th Floor, New York, NY 10019
(212) 580–6600
*www.actingstudio.com*

The Glenn Alterman Monologue/Audition Studio
400 West 43rd Street, #7G, New York, NY 10036
(212) 769–7928
*www.glennalterman.com*

Actors Institute
159 West 25th Street, New York, NY 10001
(212) 924–8888
*www.tairesources.com*

The Actors Studio Drama School
66 West 12th Street, New York, NY 10011
(212) 229-5859
*www.newschool.edu/academic/drama*

Actors Workshop
65 West 55th Street, New York, NY 10019
(212) 757-2835
(no Web site)

American Academy of Dramatic Arts
120 Madison Avenue, New York, NY 10016
(212) 686-9244
*www.aada.org*

American Musical and Dramatic Academy
2109 Broadway, New York, NY 10001
(212) 787-5300
*www.amda.edu*

Atlantic Theater Company
453 West 16th Street, New York, NY 10011
(212) 691-5919
*www.atlantictheater.org*

Cap 21
18 West 18th Street, 6th Floor, New York, NY 10011
(212) 807-0202
*www.cap21.org*

Caymichael Patten Studios
211 West 61st Street, New York, NY 10023
(212) 765-7021
*www.cpattenstudio.com*

Circle in the Square Theatre School
1633 Broadway, New York, NY 10019
(212) 307-0388
*www.circlesquare.org*

William Esper Studio, Inc.
261 West 35th Street, New York, NY 10001
(212) 904–1350
*www.esperstudio.com*

The Gene Frankel Theater
  and Film Workshop
24 Bond Street, New York, NY 10012
(212) 777–1767
*www.genefrankel.com*

Penny Templeton Studio
261 West 35th Street, Suite 304, New York, NY 10001
(212) 643–2615
*www.pennytempletonstudio.com*

Harlem Theater Company
473 West 150th Street, New York, NY 10031
(212) 281–0130
(no Web site)

H.B. Studio
120 Bank Street, New York, NY 10014
(212) 675–2370
*www.hbstudio.org*

Michael Howard Studios
152 West 25th Street, New York, NY 10010
(212) 645–1525
*www.michaelhowardstudios.com*

Kimball Studio
60 East 13th Street, New York, NY 10003
(212) 260–6373
*www.kimballstudio.com*

Lee Strasberg Theater Institute
115 East 15th Street, New York, NY 10003
(212) 533–5500
*www.strasberg.com*

Neighborhood Playhouse School of the Theatre
340 East 54th Street, New York, NY 10022
(212) 688–3770
*www.the-neiplay.org*

New Actors Workshop
259 West 30th Street, New York, NY 10001
(212) 947–1310
*www.newactorsworkshop.com*

Sande Shurin Acting Studio & Theatre
311 West 43rd Street, New York, NY 10036
(212) 262–6848
*www.sandeshurin.com*

Sally Johnson Studios
25 West 23rd Street, Floor 2, New York, NY 10010
(212) 463–7962

T. Schreiber Studio
151 West 26th Street, New York, NY 10001
(212) 741–0209
*www.t-s-s.org*

The Stella Adler Studio of Acting
31 West 27th Street, Third Floor, New York, NY 10001

The School for Film & Television
39 West 19th Street, New York, NY 10011
(212) 645–0030
*www.filmandtelevision.com*

Ward Acting Studio
145 West 28th Street, New York, NY 10001
(212) 239-1456
*www.wardstudio.com*

Weist-Barron
35 West 45th Street, New York, NY 10036
(212) 840-7025
*www.weistbarron.com*

### The Importance of Good Speech

Unfortunately, many actors arrive in New York with regionalisms or speech defects. Regionalisms can limit the types of roles an actor will be cast in. In a profession where the way that a character speaks may be of major importance, having any kind of speech impediment or regional dialect will only make your chances of landing a role more difficult. To find the best teacher for you, I suggest going through the ads in *Back Stage* listing speech teachers (especially in the classified section). Many of these teachers will require some upfront money for a number of sessions. Before you commit to this, make sure that this is the right teacher for you. Meet with the teacher and see if you feel that she can help you solve this problem. Do you feel that she is knowledgeable in this field? Do you feel that she can handle your specific problem? Try to find out who else has studied with her and what the results were. Do you feel comfortable with her? Remember, in most cases you will be working with the teacher one-on-one.

According to speech coach Sam Chwat, "People discriminate based on speech. And nowhere is this more true than in show business. Careers can be sidetracked indefinitely if an actor has an obvious speech problem."

The speech coach should be able to accurately appraise the actor's speech and be able to plan a method of working with the actors to eliminate any problem areas. Obviously, a foreign accent will have to be eliminated for an actor to play typically American roles. Actors often go to speech coaches to develop an accent needed for a specific role, say, a New York accent or a Southern accent, if the roles requires it. On occasion, an actor will need a speech coach if he has a medical condition that has impaired his speech in some way.

Mr. Chwat starts with analysis of the difference between the native and the target sounds. He then teaches the actor to imitate the new sounds in different parts of words, and shows the actor how to link words with the new sounds. He focuses more on script work for the performer who has a specific audition or script in mind, but still uses a great deal of conversational drill work, improv play, and tape-recorded assignments for the speaker who wants to permanently adopt a new manner of speaking. He carefully guides the speaker through conversational assignments, at first with low-pressure conversations, and finally in more stressful speech situations, where it might be difficult to think before speaking.

A good speech teacher will only work with the actor on speech and voice, not interpretation. Be careful of the speech coach who tries to give you line readings. Quite often, speech coaches will work with actors improvisationally to assist in using the accent more freely.

How well an actor succeeds with an accent depends on his ability to imitate, his diligence at practicing the accent, and the number of sounds necessary to change.

As Mr. Chwat says, "Actors should learn as many accents as possible to avoid typecasting and to make themselves eligible for as many roles as possible. An actor should enable himself to be seen in as many ways as possible by agents and directors, and this involves refining speech skills to suit any characterization. The Standard American English accent has been proven to be the most marketable and lucrative manner of speech for voice-over and dramatic acting, and an actor should explore every possibility of mastering this skill."

### Speech Schools and Coaches

New York Speech Improvement Services
253 West 16th Street, New York, NY 10011
(212) 242–8435
*www.nyspeech.com*

Olson Speech and Language Improvement Center
347 Fifth Avenue, Suite 1406, New York, NY 10016
(212) 951–3844
*www.olsenspeech.com*

Advanced Communication Services
201 West 16ᵗʰ Street, Suite 3E, New York, NY 10011
(212) 929–0384
*www.confidentspeech.com*

**Dance Schools**

For those actors interested in musical theater, I've listed some of the
better-known dance schools.

Alvin Ailey American Dance Center
211 West 61ˢᵗ Street, New York, NY 10023
(212) 767–0940
*www.alvinailey.org*

Ballet Arts of City Center
130 West 56ᵗʰ Street, New York, NY 10019
(212) 582–3350
*www.balart.com*

Broadway Dance Center
221 West 57ᵗʰ Street, New York, NY 10019
(212) 582–9304
*www.bdcdance.com*

Peridance Center
132 Fourth Avenue, 2ⁿᵈ Floor, New York, NY 10003
(212) 505–0886
*www.peridance.com*

Steps
2121 Broadway, New York, NY 10023
(212) 874–2410
*www.stepsnyc.com*

## Singing Teachers/Vocal Coaches

There are many singing teachers/vocal coaches in the New York City area. I've only listed a few of the better-known ones.

Paul Harman Studio
(212) 252–4767
*www.auditionsuccess.com*

Robert Marks
(212) 664–1654
*www.bobmarks.com*

Douglas J. Cohen
(212) 724–7178
georgie9L@aol.com

Lynn Starling
(212) 245–593
*starlingvoice@aol.com*

Tommy Faragher
(718) 822–8666
*tommyfaragher@aol.com*

# CHAPTER 2

# Headshots: Your Calling Card

**P**erhaps one of the most important marketing tools that actors have is the headshot. It is for that reason that several chapters of the book cover this topic. The headshot creates the first impression that casting directors, directors, and producers have of you. Hopefully your headshot expresses the image that you're trying to create for yourself. Quite often it determines the kind of auditions and work you'll be getting. It is your calling card, and an important marketing tool.

### What You See Is What You Get

Casting directors get hundreds of pictures each week. Making sure that yours stands out from the rest is very important. This eight-by-ten-inch black-and-white photo is one of the most important ingredients in your self-promotion package. But it must look like you—not the you that only exists in your imagination, not the you that's been so retouched that not one slight imperfection shows, and not the you that some photographer has lit so dramatically that all we see now are teeth and eyes, but the best *you* you can be! There is nothing more embarrassing than the look on the casting director's face when you enter her office, she looks up, and you can tell that she doesn't feel you resemble your photo in the least. Disappointment and rejection are in the wings. The photo must look like you!

Something else to keep in mind is the attitude of your picture. A pose that's too dramatic, too artsy, or too aloof will leave the casting director uninterested. What you want is a friendly, open, interesting shot. Your shoulders should be relaxed, your smile not forced. Be a strong participant in your photo session. Make sure the photographer and you are in total agreement as to what type you are, how you're marketing yourself, and what it is you're trying to say with your headshot.

### Types of Headshots

**The commercial headshot**, used for all commercial auditions, should be a photo of you smiling, preferably with teeth visible. Here's your chance to express your warmth and enthusiasm. Your photo should be saying, *Hi, I'm here and I'm confident.* Your smile should express friendliness. Your eyes, which is where most casting directors say they look first, should be warm, intelligent, and eager, *but definitely not desperate!*

**Your theatrical or "legit" headshot** should be a bit more dramatic, more relaxed. This is the photo used for submissions to theater, TV, and film. There's no need to do a hard sell here. The feeling that you should be expressing in this photo is one where you're comfortable with yourself. The casting directors and talent agents that I interviewed said they look for "aliveness, intelligence—especially in the eyes."

**The soap headshot** might be a smart investment if you're attractive, sexy, somewhat glamorous, or romantic looking (or can be). It's not really necessary, however, to have a soap shot. You can always use your theatrical (legit) photo for soaps. If you're in doubt as to what you should do, speak to your agent or a casting director about it.

**The portrait-style headshot** (a three-quarter, body shot) has become increasingly popular in the last few years. Since more of the body is shown in these photos, some casting directors prefer them, because they get a better sense of how the actor will look in person. The size of people's heads is sometimes quite different from the size and shape of their bodies. These photographs have a wide white border with a thin black line inside.

### Selecting a Photographer

Many photographers place ads in *Back Stage* and *Drama-Logue*, but I feel the best way to find a photographer is the same way you might find a doctor or lawyer: through recommendation. Ask other actors in your acting class or at auditions. Ask casting directors and agents you are in contact with who they recommend. Look at other actors' headshots. If one really impresses you, find out who the photographer was. Then ask the actor some of the following pertinent questions:

- Were you comfortable during the shoot?
- Did you feel rushed?
- Did you enjoy the shoot?
- Did you feel that you collaborated well with the photographer, or did he just give orders that you felt obliged to follow?
- Were you relaxed at the session?
- How much time did the photographer allow for the sitting?
- How much did he charge (rates can change)?

After you've gathered five to eight names of photographers, see if they have Web sites. These days, many photographers do, and you can often see a portfolio of their work and learn something about fees and scheduling before you contact them. Call them and set up appointments to meet with them and look at their portfolios. Photographers' fees for headshots range from about $150 to $850 (and higher). Price, by the way, should be only one factor in your decision-making. Getting the cheapest deal or having your headshot taken by the most "in" photographer is not the way to select a photographer. The most important consideration is how you feel with the photographer—the "vibe."

Do you feel relaxed/comfortable? Does the photographer rush the initial interview? Does he answer all your questions satisfactorily? Find out the specific financial terms of the photo shoot. The following are some questions you should keep in mind:

- How many prints will I get for the fee?
- If I want extra prints, how much will they cost?
- Does retouching/airbrushing cost extra?
- How much time do you allow for a photo session?

- Are negatives of my photos included in the price?
- How long after the session will I have to wait for my photos?
- Do you shoot outdoors?
- If I have to cancel, how much advance notice must I give to avoid being charged?

Don't be shy about asking questions. If a photographer is reluctant to answer some of your questions or you feel that he is hiding something, trust your instincts as to whether or not you should work with him.

### Looking at Portfolios

At your interview with the photographer, she should show you her portfolio. If for any reason she cannot show it to you then, arrange for a time when she can. Never book a session with any photographer unless you've seen her work! When looking at the photographer's portfolio, keep in mind the following questions.

### The Lighting

- Does the lighting have a natural look?
- Is it too dramatic?
- Do the actors' features seem washed out?
- Do the actors' skin tones seem realistic?
- Does the lighting show the contours of the actors' faces?
- Can you tell by the lighting if the actors are blonds, brunets, or redheads?
- Does the photographer use backlighting?
- Does the lighting call too much attention to itself?

### Look at the Actors

- Do they seem relaxed?
- If you were a casting director/agent looking at these photos, what would you think?
- Do you feel that the photographer got these actors to express something about themselves to you?
- Is there a sameness to all the photos?

- Do you feel this photographer works just as well with women as with men?
- Do you like the quality of this photographer's work?
- Does it seem cheaply done? Rushed?
- What's your overall feeling about the photos?

### Preparing for the Shoot

A good photographic shoot, like a good audition, will go best if you prepare well in advance. Don't wait for the last minute to make decisions. After you've selected the photographer and picked the date, you should consider the following in preparation for the shoot.

### Knowing Your Type and How to Dress

One very important aspect of being able to market yourself well is to know your "type." What type are you? Mom? Upscale? Exec? All-American? Whatever type you are, dress accordingly, but don't go overboard. Think *wardrobe*, not *costume*. Type is determined first by your physical appearance (height, weight, face, etc.). Your personality and acting ability also add into the equation. Can you convince America in thirty seconds that you are a mom and that that's your baby? Can you convince people that you're the CEO of that company? The more you know how to market your type, the more successful you'll be, especially in TV commercials and print work. Types such as college kid, young mom, executive, model, and mom and pop are just a few of the classifications used to cast commercials. Look at magazine ads and see how many different types you can find. Watch TV and notice the types used in commercials. Try to see which commercials you'd be right for.

Naturally, this does not mean that this type is all you are. You are a living, breathing, multitalented actor who has many levels and dimensions to your talent. Some actors take typecasting too personally. They feel that they are more than just a nerd or a mom. And they're right. But remember, it's just a business. Play the game and you may win. Be a maverick and you probably won't. You may also want to check with casting directors and agents that you know to ask their opinions on what type you are and how you should be marketing yourself.

Identifying costume symbols such as pins, props, jewelry, or hats should be avoided. There is nothing wrong, however, in shooting a couple of shots wearing prop glasses (as long as that works for your type).

### Tips for Women: Makeup and Hair

Women should always wear makeup at a photographic shoot. Whether you do your own makeup or you hire someone else depends on how confident you feel about it. For some actresses, just knowing that a professional stylist will take care of their makeup frees them up to deal with other aspects of the shoot. In either case, your makeup should be used just to enhance, not to hide or cover up. Always remember that your photo should look like the person who will be walking into the casting director's/agent's office. You should look like you at your best. You want your natural skin tones to show. And always remember when applying makeup that the photos are in black-and-white. If your makeup is too dramatic, it can make you look older or less attractive. In choosing lipstick colors, think of how the shade will contrast with your skin.

When considering hairstyles for headshots, you shouldn't have your hair styled too trendy. Hopefully you'll be able to use the photo for a few years. Besides, the photo shouldn't be just about hair. "Big hair" probably will take up too much focus.

### Tips for Men: Makeup and Hair

One word to keep in mind is "moderation." Many actors shave right before the shoot. It's been suggested that you shouldn't shave for a day or so before the shoot so that you'll get an especially good shave the day of the shoot. Also, use a light amount of makeup for the session. Without makeup, men's skin tends to look too washed out. As far as hairstyles, don't go overboard. As one photographer said, "Don't Elvis it up!" Not too much mousse or cream—it will make your hair greasy-looking on film.

**At the Photo Shoot**

Once the session gets underway, remember the following:

- Relax.
- You never want to seem too posed. Some feeling should always be coming from inside. Some actors actually give themselves acting tasks to keep themselves from becoming too self-conscious.
- You've heard it before, but here it is again: *Think of the camera as your friend (a close friend, an intimate friend!).*
- Legit/theater headshot and the portrait headshot: The feeling behind the photo should be one of confidence. What they're looking for is someone intelligent, interesting, exciting. Try not to make it too posed. Feel free to be spontaneous. Be expressive, courageous.
- Commercial headshot: A smile. A real smile that emanates from within. A smile that has teeth but isn't too toothy. It should be an open, enthusiastic smile. A smile that at its core stands for only one word: *Yes!*
- Soap headshot: One word: *SEX.* But not too trashy. Playful, romantic, and alluring.

# Now That the Photo Session Is Over, What Next?

**O**nce the shoot is complete, the first challenge is to pick your headshot from the contact sheet. When selecting which photo to use, keep one thing in mind: Your vote counts the most! After you've made your initial selections, bring the headshots around to actor friends, casting directors, and agents whose opinions you trust. After everyone has made his or her selections (using either different colored pencils or initialing), look at the contact sheet again—*you* have the final vote. Remember, this is your calling card. This photo represents you. Try to be subjective. Look at the photo as if it were not you, but someone you didn't know. What do you think of that person in the photo? Do you like him or her? Would you want to know him or her? What type is he or she? For some actors, being able to detach themselves and select photos can be difficult. If that's a problem for you, then I suggest you simply go along with the person whose opinion you trust the most.

### Retouching

Be careful when it comes to retouching. The tendency is to overdo it. Yes, you may remove that blemish that somehow appeared on the day of the shoot. But if it's permanent, don't get rid of it. It's part of you. If you like, you may lighten those dark, unflattering circles under your eyes that somehow appeared in the photograph but aren't part of you. If you wish, you can soften some of those lines in your face that don't normally appear but were somehow frozen in the photo. Each desired change should be carefully discussed with the photographer. Too much retouching should be avoided.

### Reproductions

After you've gotten your prints back, they've been retouched, and you're happy with them, there is one last thing to do: get repro- ductions. It would seem a shame to put all that energy into your headshot and then make inferior reproductions. At one time, many photo labs made prints from copy negatives. Today, because so many photographers shoot digitally, there are almost no traditional reproduction studios left in New York. Many reproduction studios send their materials to places outside of New York. That being said, there are still some studios that will show you their work. Here are some things to keep in mind when selecting a studio or lab to make the reproductions.

- Always look at the studio's headshot book.
- Are you pleased with the type of work they do?
- Do you like the paper they use?
- Do they answer all your questions satisfactorily?
- Do they provide test shots for you to look at (before running off the reproductions)? Do they charge extra for this service?
- Always remember that reproductions increase the contrast of your original photo. In some cases this may be flattering, but in others it can be too dramatic or unflattering.
- When selecting from the test shots, always choose the photo that is the most like your original.

### The Dos and Don'ts of Mailings

I will briefly touch on some issues to be aware of when doing your mail- ings. For further, in-depth information about mailings, see chapter 6.

- Always mail your photos in manila envelopes with cardboard inserts.
- On the envelope, print the words "DO NOT BEND." The post office is famous for mangling mailers.
- Always include a cover letter with your mailings. Included in this brief note should be a short self-introduction. Mention how you came to write to them (a friend, relative, business acquaintance, etc.).
- *Always* request an appointment. What's the point of the mailing if it's not to get to meet them in person? Tell them you'll call in a week or so. Then be sure to call them in a week or so! (More likely than not, you won't get through, but sometimes you just might, especially if they saw something in your photo or in your note that interested them.)
- If you do get through, be brief, cordial, and professional. Don't get chatty or too familiar.
- If you have a video or audiotape, mention it in your cover letter. Tell them that you'd like to have them look at it at their convenience.
- Don't write your note by hand if you have illegible handwriting. Type it instead.
- Don't guess the spelling of the name of the person to whom you are writing. Make sure it is correct. Look it up somewhere or make a phone call to find out.
- Know the sex of the person to whom you're writing. Even names like Glenn or Michael may belong to a woman.
- When writing to women, it's always safer to use "Ms." rather than "Mrs." or "Miss."
- If you don't get through when you call a couple of weeks later, wait a few days and then send a postcard politely requesting an appointment.

### Picture Postcards

Aside from headshots, you'll need a supply of picture postcards, which you can get from the reproduction studio when you have your headshots made. As with your headshot, you should list your name, union affiliations, and contact numbers under the photo on the front of the card. Most often, actors select their commercial headshot for the postcard, too. Whichever photo you use, it should be friendly, open, and able to capture the eye of the receiver. Many actors overdo postcard mailings.

Postcards are best used to inform casting directors and agents about progress in your career, to thank them for a job they recently hired you for, or sometimes to include in the envelope with fliers for shows you're presently performing in. I know of a few actors who mail their postcards in envelopes, paying the regular mail rate rather than the postcard rate. Their thinking is that a casting director will be more likely to look at a postcard in an envelope (as opposed to the hundreds of other postcards they receive each week). It's up to you and your budget.

If you're about to appear on a soap or in a movie, use the postcard to announce your news. They should not be sent too often. If you want to, using them once a month just to say hello is fine. More than that is a waste of time, energy, and postage.

### Photo Business Cards

Photo business cards are handy, economical, and a great marketing tool. You never know when you'll meet a casting director or agent. Since you're not always carrying a picture and resume with you, this small photo business card, carried conveniently in your wallet, is an excellent way to give them your contact information. The photo business can be an important networking tool. For that casting director or agent that you meet at the theater who wants to know how to contact you, just hand him your card with your contact information. You can have these cards made when you have your headshots.

### Color!

Color headshots are starting to become popular in New York, though they've been popular in Los Angeles for the last few years. Color adds a whole new dimension to your headshot. They are especially useful for redheads, blonds, and people of color. Although color reproductions cost a bit more, they're well worth it. More and more photographers are now shooting in color.

### Photo Reproduction Studios

What follows are some of the more popular photo reproduction companies. Some are in New York City; others, you mail your photos to and they mail back your reproductions. Generally these mail companies cost quite a bit less, but you may have to wait up to two weeks for your finished photos.

Precision Photos
750 Eighth Avenue, New York, NY 10036
(212) 302–2724
(800) 583–4077
*www.precisionphotos.com*

ABC Pictures
1867 E. Florida Street, Springfield, MO 65803–4583
(888) 526–5336
*www.abcpictures.com*

Modernage Photographic Services Inc.
1150 Sixth Avenue, New York, NY 10036
(212) 997–1800
*www.modernage.com/headshots_index.html*

Reproductions
6 West 37th Street, New York, NY 10036
(212) 967–2568
*www.reproductions.com*

For postcards, you can contact the above reproduction companies or try 1–800-Postcards at:
1–800-Postcards
121 Varick Street, 3rd Floor, New York, NY 10013
(212) 741–1070
*www.1800postcards.com*

# Interviews with Photographers and Reproduction Studio Owners

## The Photographers

ARTHUR COHEN (**AC**) has been a photographer in New York City for about seventeen years. He has photographed many celebrities but prefers to keep his client list private. He also works for a number of different magazines, shoots album covers, and does photo editorials.

JINSEY DAUK (**JD**) has her work represented in most casts of Broadway shows today. She has been a celebrity photographer for many years. She shot all the new models at such agencies as Ford and Elite for several years. Her specialty is that she brings "naturalism" to headshots by not using a flash in her photo sessions.

ROBERT KIM (**RK**) has been a celebrity photographer for over twenty-five years, with studios in Los Angeles and New York. He is also a working actor, so his experience on both sides of the camera have made him a sought-after keynote speaker. His speeches place an emphasis on photography for the working actor.

**What would you say are the most common mistakes actors make at a photo session?**

**AC**: The most common mistake is the one they make before the photo session: their marketing plans, their types. Not knowing how to market themselves is major. If you don't know what type you are, then you can't make the right decisions as to what to wear, your hair, your look, etc. Other mistakes include coming in for a shooting after getting a bad haircut, bringing the wrong clothes, or getting head-shots before you're ready.

**JD**: The thing that bothers me the most is when I feel the actors don't seem to care. Perhaps they got the session as a gift, or whatever. What I'll feel is that there is no collaboration with me. Perhaps they're just feeling insecure or cut-off emotionally, but the energy is dead. It makes my job very hard.

**RK**: The most common mistake actors make is simply this: *Choosing the wrong photographer*. If you've chosen the right one in the first place, everything should go well, and you'll end up with spectacular photographs. If you've chosen poorly, nothing you do during your session will noticeably improve the outcome. If the actor has done his homework, and selected a headshot photographer who truly knows his craft and thoroughly understands the special needs of the actor, there really isn't any single mistake that an actor can make during a session that can't be easily corrected by a competent photographer.

**What criteria do you feel actors should use when selecting a photographer?**

**AC**: You should ask yourself, Do you like this photographer's style? Do you like the photographer? Are you comfortable in the studio? Does the photographer come highly recommended? Bottom line—it should be a visceral, gut feeling that this photographer is right for you.

**JD**: They have to see a warmth in the photographer's pic-tures when they're looking at his or her portfolio. They should, most importantly, feel some kind of connection with the photographer.

**RK**: Use the same guidelines that you'd use to intelligently select *any* top professional. For example, what are his credentials? How long has he been in business? Is he published? Who recommends him? Look for a photographer with a proven track record of marketing many successful actors, not the "new kid on the block" or some guy who'll shoot your new headshots for free "to build up his portfolio." The three most important words in selecting a good photographer are: *compare, compare, compare*. You should always visit the photographer's studio first, and compare his work with the others'. You may want to compile a list by getting recommendations from your fellow actors, or agents, managers, acting coaches, and casting directors. Also, be sure to look through several popular actors' publications or visit a variety of headshot photographers' Web sites, such as Reproductions, to help you narrow down your choices. Then make an appointment to see their books. It may be time-consuming, but it remains the only true way of determining a photographer's ability. Never take anyone else's word for how good a photographer is, they may know less than you! And *never* make your final decision based solely upon price.

### How can actors prepare for a shoot?

**AC**: Again, marketing is the best way you can prepare. Be in as good a shape as you can be. Know who you are and what it is that makes you unique.

**JD**: Bringing your own music can be of some help. Bring something that relaxes you, that can get you ready to play. If you're nervous, *that's good*! We can use that energy. Iron your clothes. Make sure your nails are clean and even in length.

**RK**: A photo session isn't a play. It doesn't require weeks of intense scene study, rehearsal, blocking, sound tests, or dress rehearsals. All the actor needs to do is get sufficient rest, and make sure that the person he's finally settled on understands *exactly* what it is he wants to achieve in the session before he comes in for the sitting. The rest is up to the photographer.

**What type and how much wardrobe do you recommend actors bring to the shoot?**

**AC**: I like to do four or five really good changes. They should be clothes you love and are really comfortable in. The clothes should reflect both your type and personality.

**JD**: I usually feel that you should bring eleven or twelve things, and then when you get here, we can go through the clothes together. More is better than less. Clothes should direct all the attention to your face. Solid-colored things work best. Bright white doesn't, black does. Textures are wonderful. The most effective headshots are ones where the clothes are secondary and we're not aware of what you're wearing.

**RK**: Whenever I see photographers who routinely hand their clients a prewritten list of "Things to Wear in a Photo Shoot," I cringe. What this shows is that a photographer is either too lazy to help the actor determine the specific wardrobe choices that will make the session a success, or too uninformed to know anything about clothing and it's important role in headshot photography. Proper wardrobe selection, much like acting instruction, is a highly individual thing, and must be given every bit as much care. In all cases, the appropriate wardrobe should always be thought out well in advance, and tailored to achieve the actor's specific needs prior to the shoot. But when in doubt, *it's better to bring too many clothes, rather than not enough.*

**Any cosmetic tips for men and women at a shoot?**

**AC**: Don't have a heavy tan or you'll photograph muddy. Make sure your hair is exactly the right length and color before the shoot. At some times of the year, some people's skin is drier and flakier; don't shoot then (unless you've taken care of it with humidifiers and moisturizers). If your hair is damaged in the summer, make sure to take care of that before the session. I like people to be close to their ideal weight. If you're going to have any cosmetic dental work, make sure you're comfortable with how it feels before you set up a photo session.

**JD**: The rule of thumb here is whatever you see in the mirror is exactly what you're going to get. Women should come to the shoot with their hair and makeup already done. They can do last-minute stuff right before the shoot. Men—wear no makeup. Blending makeup is very important; otherwise you'll look like a Fellini clown on film. Women should use two powder puffs to blend foundation, blush, and powder together.

**RK**: Makeup should be under the direct supervision of the photographer, and never left up to the actor (unless the actor is a seasoned professional makeup artist, which most are not). Both men and women require makeup. It should be provided by the photographer, not left up to the actor.

**How often do you feel actors should get new headshots?**

**AC**: Not until you've changed substantially from your last headshot.

**JD**: Probably every eight years. Unless the actor has changed a lot. If he's lost a lot of weight or changed his hair, then perhaps sooner.

**RK**: You can quote me on my next words of advice, because I've spent most of my adult life thinking about it. I believe that the only time an actor needs new headshots are when one or both of these two factors are present:
1) When your old headshots are no longer working.
2) When your looks have changed so drastically that your photograph no longer looks like you (i.e., you've visibly aged, you've changed your hairstyle or color, gained or lost weight, etc.).
Arbitrary rules like "every six months" or "every year" are, in my opinion, a lot of hooey, no doubt promoted by greedy headshot photographers. There's an old saying: "If it ain't broke, don't fix it."

That being said, if your current headshots aren't booking you auditions or promoting you properly, don't even hesitate. Get a new one.

**What should actors be thinking during the shoot? Is there something that they can focus on to help make their pictures look more alive?**

**AC**: I work very easy when I shoot, very conversational. If they want some more dramatic shots, I'll ask them to run a little monologue in their brain. I'm not a real "coacher." I'm more relaxed in the way I work.

**JD**: It's not an acting exercise. You have to be willing to allow the photographer to direct you. The more you can play into his or her directions, relax and just go with the moment, the better your pictures will come out. Mainly we aim for spontaneity in each picture. Aliveness. I usually tell my clients to close their eyes and think about something funny. When they open their eyes, I start shooting. Remember, the casting director wants to feel the life, the spirit, come through in the photo.

**RK**: Every actor is entirely unique and different, and therefore, no single pat rule about "what to think" is pertinent to creating a successful headshot session. *It is the direct responsibility of the photographer* to create the various scenarios that will help his subject focus better. But if your photographer doesn't have a clear vision of exactly what he wants to accomplish in the session in the first place, the actor may have difficulty getting to the correct emotion, and his headshots will suffer.

**Specifically regarding your studio: What is included in a session? How many pictures are taken?**

**AC**: Two unretouched eight-by-tens, four rolls of film (144 shots). I also do Polaroid previews.

**JD**: I shoot three rolls (each roll has thirty-six exposures).

**RK**: I've been 100 percent digital for three years now. I simply keep shooting until both the actor and I feel totally confident that we've "got it." There isn't any annoying need to stop when the camera runs out of film or when "you're on a roll"—one of the many benefits of shooting digitally.

### How much time does each session take?

**AC**: I allow four hours, but generally, my male sessions are two hours, my female sessions are three.

**JD**: I allow two hours for each session. Since I don't use flash, there is no lost time (or energy) to my sessions.

**RK**: The answer to that question is: *As long as it takes.*

I normally shoot only two actors a day, giving me more than enough time to shoot a session of any size. Since every actor is different, I never, ever place an arbitrary time limit on anyone.

### How much in advance do you need to book a session?

**AC**: Right now it's six weeks, but typically, it's two months in advance.

**JD**: It depends. Anywhere from two weeks to a month.

**RK**: That depends totally on my workload, which varies from season to season. L.A. tends to be more film- and episodic-television-oriented, and New York, more theater, which is why I maintain studios on both coasts. I shoot seven days a week.

---

### The Photo Reproduction Studio Owners

CAMERON STEWART (**CS**) is the owner of Reproductions. He's been in the photographic field for twenty-one years and at Reproductions for seven.

MIKE CANIZARES (**MC**) is the owner of Precision Photos. He has been in this field for twenty-two years.

---

**In selecting a photo reproduction studio, what things should an actor look for?**

**CS**: Quality, service, and a willingness of the lab to work with them and help them. Pictures are, in a sense, an advertising piece. Actors should ask the photographer they're working with to suggest a reproduction lab. Since they've hired the photographer as a technical professional, they should trust his advice. Also, in the theatrical community, there is a tremendous amount of word of mouth going around.

**MC**: Generally, they should look for a combination of the following:
Quality. Photographic copies are an accurate copy to your original. Allow for a small quality loss.
Pricing. Hey, we all know 99 percent of actors working diligently understand why it's called "show *business*"!
Turnaround Time. You'll be amazed how many clients I've encountered that have procrastinated and need pics in a hurry.
Retouching Services. It's an excellent convenience to have retouching services on-site. Pricing should range from $25 to $35 for excellent retouching.

**What are the common problems actors make when bringing in their photos?**

**CS**: I think the most important thing is actors should realize is that this is a business. Many actors come in and go at this in sort of a half-hearted sense. Consequently, we have actors come in and buy like fifty copies of their photos, something like that. In a sense, they're wasting their money. Fifty copies aren't going to get you very far. You need to work with extensive mailings, get your name out there. In order to do that, you need to work with a greater volume of pictures, which also consequently goes to a lower per-unit value. Look at it as an investment in copies as an advertising venture in a business.

**MC**: Expectations that the copies should look EXACTLY like the original. Since it is a second-generation image, there is always going to be a loss of finite detail. These days, however, with many photographers shooting digitally, this isn't true; the quality is almost identical.

Bringing in a photo that is either of poor quality (bad focus, smaller than 8 × 10 size).

I've encountered problems with some photographers supplying their clients with "inkjet quality" photographs. Inkjet paper is very susceptible to scratches and, if they're not printed properly, you can see the inkjet dots on the original.

## What should actors expect and not expect from reproductions?

**CS**: Actors must be prepared for the subtle differences between their original and the reproduction copies. Sometimes actors expect an exact match.

**MC**: Actors should expect that their photocopies will have slight changes from the original. There's always a slight loss of detail, since you're printing from a first-generation image to a second-generation one.

## Any suggestions you have regarding eight-by-tens and postcards?

**CS**: You must scrutinize the original photo before giving it to a lab. Too often, actors will select a photo without looking at the photo's details. Then, after you've made up a hundred copies, you realize that there are little distracting things that you never considered. Look carefully at those atmospheric features in the background. Something might be more distracting than you realize.

**MC**: Eight-by-tens are the definitive tool in marketing and a staple (no pun intended) of the entertainment industry.

Postcards are excellent tools in a few ways. Their versatility is an advantage when trying to get the word out about yourself or performances. Two images on a postcard can show two completely different sides of an actor (i.e., man clean-shaven/full beard, woman in business suit/mom dressed down with kids).

**Any other photo items actors can use for self-promotion?**

**CS**: Photo reproductions are also used for voice-over cassette covers and opening announcements for plays and nightclub acts. One thing I always suggest is to know your audience. That is, know who you're targeting and find the best tool, be it a photo or whatever, to get their attention.

**MC**: I suggest photo business cards as an excellent tool to network yourself. A nice, down-to-earth headshot or three-quarter shot (unless you are marketing yourself otherwise). They are less cumbersome than postcards. Also, the way you personalize it by designing the layout of your name and information states a lot about you.

# *Resumes*

**A**n actor's resume is quite different from a business resume, in both content and format. Knowing what and what not to put on the resume is very important. The resume should be professional-looking and to the point. Simply put, you should list whatever experience (professional or showcase) you've had, who you've trained with, and where. The resume should never be handwritten. Have it typed professionally and check it carefully for typos.

The resume is *attached* to the back of your picture. I emphasize the word "attached" because so often, resumes are poorly attached and fall off, leaving your picture stranded. When the casting director/agent turns your picture over, guess what? There's nothing there. Into the garbage can your picture goes. To avoid this, carefully staple or glue the photo to the back of your resume. Some actors actually have their resumes copied directly to the back of their photos. There's certainly no chance of it ever getting lost that way. No matter what, make sure that your resume fits properly on the picture. If it's too big, the edges will get torn or curled.

### What to Include on Your Resume

All the casting directors I interviewed were very clear about what they want to see on a resume. They want to know "the truth, the whole truth, and nothing . . ."

But if your experience is limited, is it okay to fudge a bit? Let me just say that many actors do. Not big lies, but little ones. It's certainly not too bright to claim you've played the Phantom in *The Phantom of the Opera* on Broadway if you haven't. Some casting directors are immediately turned off if they detect even a little lie. A major pet peeve of many casting directors is misspellings. The information should be listed by category (not randomly). Some casting directors have suggested using an off-white color paper (such as beige) because it cuts down on the glare from harsh office lights. This may be an unnecessary expense. It's up to you.

### The Format and Order of Information

Your resume should only be one page long. It should be neatly printed, well organized, and well typed. The following information should appear exactly the same on either a New York resume or a Los Angeles resume.

### The Heading

- First of all, your name should be at the top. It should be in a different font or style from the rest of the text below.
- If you belong to any performing unions, you should list them directly below your name.
- A few spaces down, on the left-hand side of the page, you should list a telephone number where you can be reached, a beeper number, or an answering service number. Since you really never know where your resume will end up, it's suggested that you don't list your home phone number.
- On the right-hand side of the page, directly across from your telephone number, list your height.
- Below your height, list your weight; below that, your hair color; below that, the color of your eyes.
- If you are a singer or dancer, include the pertinent information (voice type and what type of dancing you do).

## Example of the Heading on Top of an Actor's Resume

# JOE ACTOR
# (SAG AFTRA AEA)

| | |
|---|---|
| Beeper: (212) 769–2247 | Height: 6'1" |
| Answering Machine: (212) 967–5540 | Weight: 182 |
| Diane Arnsly Talent Agency | Hair: Brown |
| Agent's Phone: (212) 655–8876 | Eyes: Hazel |

## The Body of the Resume

The main difference between the New York resume and the Los Angeles resume is the emphasis on certain credits. In Los Angeles, which is mostly a movie and TV town, casting directors want to know what films and episodic TV work you've done. In New York City (and Chicago), they are more interested in what theater work you've done and who you've trained with.

## The New York Resume

### Order of Necessary Information

- *Theater credits* are usually listed first. Name the play, your role, and the theater. Under the theater category you should list whether you worked on Broadway, Off-Broadway, or in regional theater. Some actors list the directors with whom they've worked (especially if they're well known).
- Next, list any *film credits* you have. Include each film's title and the role you played (including whether it was a leading role, featured role, or supporting role).
- Beneath this category you should list any *television credits* you have, including the show's title and the character's name.
- In the *commercial* category, which is next, it is not necessary to list all the TV and radio spots that you've done. All they need to know is whether you've done on-camera and/or voice-over work and whether or not you have a reel. Most people usually state, "list available upon request."

- *Training* should include the type of training you received (acting, voice, speech, dance), and the teacher's name and/or school.
- List any *special skills* that you have, such as marathon runner, yoga instructor, and/or any language that you speak fluently.

**Example of the New York Resume**

# LAURENCE APPLETON

| | |
|---|---|
| Service: (212) 769- 2320 | Height: 6'1" |
| Agent: Steven Drucker Talent | Weight: 175 |
| Agent's Phone Number: (212) 777–6687 | Hair: Brown |
| | Eyes: Hazel |

THEATER

| | | | |
|---|---|---|---|
| Off-Broadway | *As Is* | Saul | Circle Rep. |
| | *My Life* | Paul | Soho Rep. |
| Regional | *Men in White* | Pete | George St. Playhouse (East Brunswick, New Jersey) |
| | *The Zoo Story* | Jerry | Yale Rep. Theater |
| TELEVISION | *Loving* | Steve | ABC-TV (recurring) |

COMMERCIALS   Have done on-camera principals—over 45 national network and regional spots (tape available upon request)

TRAINING   Acting: Scene Study with Uta Hagen (H.B. Studio)
Voice: Ed Dixon
Speech: Merilee Nolan

SPECIAL SKILLS   Yoga instructor, marathon runner, speak French

### The Los Angeles Resume

#### Order of Necessary Information

The main difference between the resume of the actor seeking work in Los Angeles rather than in New York City is placement of categories. (For a definition of each category, see the New York Resume: Order of Necessary Information, above.)

- *Film* experience should be listed first.
- *Television* is next.
- *Commercials* ("list available upon request").
- *Theater* is listed below that.
- *Training* is next.
- *Special skills* are listed last.

#### Example of the Los Angeles Resume

## INA SMALL

Service: (213) 769–7789                                        Height: 5'5"
                                                               Weight: 140
                                                               Hair: Red
                                                               Eyes: Blue

FILM

| *Queen of the Valley* | Roma (lead) | Red Eye Films |

TELEVISION

| *Murphy Brown* | Ann Leard (guest star) | CBS-TV |
| *Seaquest* | Mila (featured role) | NBC-TV |

THEATER

| *Barefoot in the Park* Corie | | Weathervane Theater |
| *Promises, Promises* Fran Kubelik | | Hempstead Playhouse |

COMMERCIALS
On-camera principals—national network spots (list available upon request)

TRAINING
Acting: Terry Schreiber (3 years), Larry Moss (2 years)
Speech: Lee Kristen
Dance: Steve Kallens (jazz)

SPECIAL SKILLS
Gymnastics, marathon runner, speak fluent French and Italian

### Photo Stills from Shows You've Worked On

Something that is becoming increasing popular these days, and that I recommend to all of my students, is exhibiting small photos (stills) of you taken from shows, films, or sometimes even commercials you've done (if it's very "character"), right on your resume. These 1/2 inch or so photos are scanned through a computer and lined up down the right hand side margin of your resume. You can fit up to five or six of them on a resume. They should show you playing different types of roles. These photos can show your range as actor. There is computer software now that can freeze a still from a commercial or film you've done. Most plays have a still photographer who takes publicity photos. You'll want to contact that photographer and see if you can get a copy of at least one good shot where you are actively engaged in a scene. When casting directors, agents, and directors look at your resume, their eyes will immediately go to the photos first. When casting directors see you playing a variety of roles, several things might go through their minds. First, that you're an actor who is working. Next, that you are a versatile actor. And finally, it might give them the idea to call you in for a role that they hadn't thought you could play.

### Listing Review Excerpts (Blurbs)

Another attention-getter that is starting to appear on resumes is a list of a few short blurbs from reviews of you (not the show) on the left-hand side of the resume. You'll want to list the most impressive lines from the most acknowledged critics. Naturally, it would be great if you can get a mention from the *New York Times*. But even if it's from a local paper, the blurb will have some value if it points out the merits of your performance. I know it might seem like you don't have much room on your resume for your credits if you have both photos on the right side and the reviews on the left, but I've seen it done attractively, and it doesn't have to use up too much space. Vary the font sizes so that it's easy on the eye. You may also just list the reviews or the stills.

### For Actors with Little or No Professional Experience

If you've just gotten out of school or have had little professional experience, it's best not to lie about it. You should include a paragraph or two in your cover letter telling the agent about the work you've done in school (school productions or community theater). It's perfectly okay to share your enthusiasm and determination in the letter, but always keep the tone professional, never desperate.

It might go something like this:

I've been in New York City for less than a year. Prior to coming here, I studied theater at Emerson College in Boston. I received a degree in Theater Arts. While at Emerson, I played the lead in *Peer Gynt* for our junior year main-stage production. In my senior year, I played Tony in *West Side Story*. I also worked at the Theater Company of Boston as an apprentice.

I am presently studying acting with Gene Frankel at the Gene Frankel Theatre and Film Workshop, singing with Charles Dewinn at the Elonard Conservatory, and taking a dance class (jazz technique) at Luigi's. Since arriving here, I've done two showcases. I played Jimmy Porter in *Look Back in Anger* (A.T.A. Theater) and Renauld in *The Crazy Cages*, a new play, at Theater for the New City. I've enclosed some reviews of my work for your consideration.

I feel strongly that if I can get the auditions, I can book the jobs. I'm ready to be sent out. I'd like to meet with you at your earliest convenience to discuss representation. I'll call you at your office at the beginning of the week. I look forward to meeting with you.

### Resume Services

Many actors do not have access to a computer or are not computer savvy. For them, creating a resume can be a real chore. Fortunately, there are now quite a few companies that help actors create their resumes (and create showcase flyers and promotional pictures). Shakespeare Mailing is one, Plaza Desktop Publishing, another. For this book, I met with Doug Barron of Plaza Desktop Publishing to discuss what a resume service like his company should provide for an actor.

Plaza Desktop Publishing (*www.plazadesktoppublishing.com*) is a small, personal desktop publishing and graphic design company that specializes in designs for the theatrical community. Mr. Barron originally started his business by creating resumes for actors, a service he continues today. As Mr. Barron states, "Resumes should be clear and easy to read, and they should highlight an actor's strengths." As an actor who has worked on resumes with many top agencies, Mr. Barron can help the actor to decide what should actually go on the resume. If you're signed with a talent agent, the agency's logo should be placed on the resumes as well, eliminating the need to use stickers, thus saving valuable time.

Other Resume Services:
Talent Search at Shakespeare Mailing
311 West 43rd Street, 4th Floor, New York, NY 10017
*www.shakespearemailing.com*

Professional Resumes
60 East 42nd Street, Suite 839, New York, NY 10165
*www.proresume.com*

Plaza Desktop Publishing
484 West 43rd Street, New York, NY 10036
212-947-1608
*www.plazadesktoppublishing.com*

### Answering Services and Pagers

An actor must be able to be contacted 24/7, for auditions as well as for work. Many casting directors and agents will call an alternate actor if the one they were trying to reach cannot be contacted. Give your personal phone numbers to agents and casting directors you know. I strongly suggest that you don't have your home phone number (or address) on your resume. You never know who will have access to this information.

What follows is a listing of some of the better answering services and pager companies.

Actorfone
545 Eighth Avenue, Room 40, New York, NY 10018
(212) 502–0666
*www.efls.com*

Bells Are Ringing
545 Eighth Avenue, Suite 401, New York, NY 10018
(212) 714–3888
*www.efls.com*

Aardvark Answering Service
545 Eighth Avenue, Suite 401
New York, NY 10018
(212) 626–9000
*www.efls.com*

# Mailing Campaigns and Promotional Marketing

**M**ailing campaigns are one of the ways actors can get in touch with casting directors and talent agents to make initial contact and pursue future work. Industry people prefer not to have their day interrupted by phone calls and visits from actors, so the mailing campaign is one practical solution. The initial mailing should include a well thought-out cover letter, a recent photo (that really looks like you!), and a well-organized resume. You should keep an updated file of who you have made contact with and maintain future correspondence on a regular basis, especially when you've booked a job or can be seen in a show in town. Don't overdo mailings. There's a fine line between keeping in touch and making a nuisance of yourself.

## Getting Your Word Out

Many actors do not have the time, the patience, or the discipline necessary to maintain an ongoing weekly or monthly mailing campaign and hire promotional marketing companies to keep their campaigns going.

According to Michael Neeley, who has worked extensively with actors in this area, "The majority of actors will try a mailing (large or small) one time. If they don't get dramatic results, they never do it again. Then they wonder why their career becomes stagnant, why they can't seem to get an agent or a job."

According to Neeley, "Most actors, at one time or another, have seen a performance for which they would have been a better casting choice, both in talent and type. What separates the actor that got the role from the actor that was 'right' for the role? There's a good chance that it boiled down to mailings."

A good mailing is sent to all the casting directors and agents that you'd like to meet. It is made up of your picture and resume and a professional, cordial, and interesting cover letter.

### What a Good Cover Letter Is and What It Can Do for You

Hal Hochhauser, the owner of Shakespeare Mailing Service, says, "The headshot shows what you look like and the resume lists related background and experience. Very important items, but on their own, they can create a somewhat impersonal appearance, considering the personal nature of our business and the importance of this introduction. It's the cover letter that gives you a voice, a personality, and a chance to convey your thoughts."

In the absence of personal contact, the cover letter becomes your smile, your sincerity, and your way to talk to the buyers and sellers of talent. It's an opportunity to share information that may not be on your resume, or to highlight important achievements that might be missed as they hastily scan the resumes that cross their desks every day. It's a chance to help strangers know your career path, understand your motivations and commitments, develop rapport with you, and perhaps be motivated to call you for a personal meeting or audition.

The cover letter also answers many unasked questions that agents and casting directors might have, such as: Is this person intelligent, focused, realistic, and understanding of the business? Are her thoughts scattered, her expectations based on fantasy, and her presentation sloppy and poorly thought out? A good cover letter conveys a lot and can be as important to the success of a mailing as the picture and resume themselves.

People tend to work with people they like, and good communication can facilitate your ability to create good business relationships. A personalized letter becomes a one-to-one communication that can make your reader feel important and your message more meaningful and influential. It tells the reader you recognize his value to your career and it maximizes your chance of getting a response.

### What Should Be Included in a Good Cover Letter

A good cover letter should be direct, professional, cordial, and succinct. The following information should be provided for casting directors and agents:

- State what it is you want, why you're writing this letter.
- Briefly tell them a bit about what you've been doing recently, highlighting important successes (especially those not obviously listed on your resume).
- Don't tell them the story of your life!
- Briefly let them know your goals, future plans, and expectations. (Naturally, you should keep this positive and upbeat, with realistic goals.)
- If you have made some good casting director contacts while seeking work, feel free to attach a note with their names. (Tell the truth, they may call them!)
- As you complete the letter, mention that you will call them sometime in the next week to arrange an appointment (and do that!).
- End your letter with an expression such as, "With warm regards" or "Sincerely."

## An Example of a Good Cover Letter

June 14, 2005

Contact name
Agency name
Address
City, State, Zip

Dear Ms. So-and-So,

I am currently seeking new representation, and would like to meet with you to discuss the possibility of working with you. Although I presently have commercial representation (freelancing with Cunningham, Escott, Dipene and Associates), I would consider signing across the board if that is your agency's policy.

There are two important issues I would like to mention that are not apparent on my resume. First of all, I have been making my living as an actor for the last couple of years. In addition, in the short time that I've been in New York City, I have been developing. Many of the interviews and auditions I get are through personal sources. Ninety percent of the work that I book is through my own efforts. I don't say this to downplay the need for representation, but rather to express to you my personal motivation and aggressiveness. I firmly believe that, with your representation, I would be able to earn a six-figure income. There are simply too many audition opportunities passing me by.

On that note and for your reference, I have attached a list of the casting directors/offices that are familiar with my work.

I will follow up with a phone call next week to arrange an appointment. If that is inconvenient, or if you would like to meet sooner, please don't hesitate to contact me. I look forward to speaking with you in person.

With warm regards,

The Actor

### The Value of Postcards in Your Ongoing Mailings

Generally, actors will get more work from their postcard mailings than from their headshots. According to Hal Hochhauser at Shakespeare Mailing Service, the reason for this is that "postcards are mailed more frequently. Agents and casting directors often tell you to keep in touch with them by postcards. They (postcards) cost less to mail than eight-by-tens and are less expensive to reproduce; you save on envelopes and postage; they're easier to prepare—no gluing, stapling, stuffing, or sealing; and, most importantly, they're handled better by agents and casting directors.

"Offices get so much mail that they cannot physically save and file pictures/resumes that aren't used. Compared to post-cards, they're cumbersome to manage and take up a lot of room. Postcards are small and can easily be stacked on a shelf or stored in a drawer. Some agents/casting directors keep catego-rized card files on their desks. When a specific type is sought, they just thumb though the cards, pulling out any that may be appropriate. Compared to your eight-by-ten, your postcard stands a better chance of being saved, thereby increasing your chance of being called at some future date from a picture you send today.

"Regular mailings, with messages that highlight your qualifica-tions and experience, keep your face familiar and phone number handy, increasing the chance of being called when someone of your type is needed."

### What to Say on Your Postcard

- Make sure it's properly addressed, with the correct spelling of the casting director's name.
- Keep it legible.
- Keep it very brief.
- Make it friendly but businesslike (not too personal).
- Always sign your card.

### Examples of Postcard Notes

Dear Jane,
I am presently touring nationally
with *Cats*. We hit Chicago this
week. Hope all is well in NYC.        Jane Doe Casting
I will be back in town in late May.   115 South Street
                                      Suite 205
All my best,                          New York, NY 10036
Joan

Dear Ms. Doe,
I just wanted to keep you posted on my latest work. I recently
completed my demo reel, which included footage from *Law and
Order*, *Hope and Faith*, and *All My Children*.
    If you'd like to view it, please give me a call.

All the best,

Bernie

### The Marketing Aspect of Actor Mailings

Repetition and frequency are essential elements in all successful
advertising. Any marketing professional can tell you that it's a "numbers business." You have to increase the public awareness to sell the
product. The "public" in this case is casting directors and agents,
while the "product"" is the actor. Coca-Cola is a household name. Yet,
The Coca-Cola Company still advertises because it knows that
buyers' needs change on a daily basis. The product needs to be
constantly in their faces. What Coca-Cola is saying is, "Yes, you have
other options—but drink Coke." Actors are saying, by their constant
reminders, "Think of me. Remember me. Use me."
    It's been said that casting directors only forget about you if you
let them. Two very simple promotional tools are constantly in effect

during the actor's mailings: (1) product recognition—casting directors must know who you are; and (2) product credibility—through your constant mailings to them, you become more viable.

Casting director Shannon Klassel of Donald Case Casting states, "We cast many jobs, such as MTV promos and other projects calling for new faces, from photos sent directly to our office. Any actor, particularly one new to the business, who doesn't do his or her mailings on a regular basis isn't tending to his or her career."

In the words of the great Milton Berle, "If opportunity doesn't knock, build a door."

### Grassroots Publicists

The following promotional marketing companies are experienced in helping actors with their mailing campaigns.

Shakespeare Mailing Service
311 West 43rd Street, New York, NY 10036
(212) 956-MAIL
*www.shakespearemailing.com*

This company has been in business for over eighteen years. It has more than five thousand clients and an office staff of about ten. The service does mailings from its contact lists or yours. It sets up various lists according to the actor's specific needs (for example, List A for New York agents, B for regional theaters, and C for L.A.) and has different mailing schedules or messages for each. Industry movement is tracked by computer to help keep your file current. The company also assists actors in creating that all-important cover letter. According to owner Hal Hochhauser, "The headshot and resume are a perfect representation of who you are and what you've done, but they're static. We help you create a personalized cover letter that bridges the gap and connects you to the specific casting director. You should follow that initial resume/headshot campaign with postcards on a regular basis. As you know, each casting director receives sometimes hundreds of pieces of mail a day. You only have two to six seconds to catch that agent's or casting director's eye. We help actors with their postcards as well. Our clients book more work more often from postcard mailings (as compared to headshot mailings)."

TVI Actors Studio
14429 Ventura Blvd., Suite 118, Sherman Oaks, CA, 91423
(818) 784–6500
Also at:
165 West 43rd, New York, NY 10036
(212) 302–1900
*www.tvistudios.com*

Owner Alan Nusbaum was a talent agent for Cunningham, Escott, Dipene and Associates for almost a decade. He noticed how misguided actors were about the business side of the entertainment industry. He set up TVI (Talent Ventures Incorporated) out of that need. TVI puts together resumes and cover letters for members, and provides them with up-to-date industry mailing lists and labels. Actors are drilled on the names of casting directors, and are advised on matters such as headshots and postcards. They can attend casting seminars and are provided with rehearsal space for practices. TVI also schedules a yearly talent tour called "Broadway to Hollywood," in which actors go to Los Angeles for one week and audition in front of thirty casting directors.

Henderson's Mailing Labels
360 East 65th Street, New York, NY 10021
(212) 472–2292
*www.hendersonenterprises.com*

Sue Henderson created this company in 1983 and says it's the "original" actor mailing label list company. Her lists include: Major Mailer—all casting directors in New York, including soaps, series, independent casting directors, ad agencies, and production houses that keep files (there are also smaller versions of this list); New York Soaps; Casting Directors; Production Companies; Model Commercial Print; and Photographers. Henderson also has a service called Mailing List Setup that allows you to create your own list using her database.

# *Personal Marketing*

In his book *How to Market Yourself*, Michael Dainard defines marketing as "a social and managerial process by which individuals and groups obtain what they need and want through creating and exchanging products and value with others." Dainard says that "marketing has been with us since the beginning of human existence. Whenever you have two or more human beings together, competition sets in and someone starts trying to market something to one of the others. The first recorded example of brilliant marketing, though not necessarily of a good product, took place in the Garden of Eden, when the serpent convinced Eve to try the apple. Eve in turn marketed the apple to Adam."

Dainard points out that "as children, we start doing our test marketing very early. We try different forms of persuasion until we find the ones that work best for us. Then we try our early successes on our other family members and friends. Sometimes we find out these strategies don't work on all people at all times, and have to develop new ones for different people and situations.

"This is an early and valuable marketing lesson. We have to use different marketing techniques on different people to get what we want. When we grow older, we use forms of marketing to get a girl/boyfriend or a wife/husband. Are we not using marketing tools when we dress up to impress and win the target of our affections (packaging)? What about the words and speeches we use (audio)? The flowers, candies, movies, and presents (promotion)?"

### Actor "Product" Marketing

Lee K. Bohlen, a professional life coach, who holds workshops for actors, says it's "very important that actors think of themselves as a 'product.' Once they do, they must then figure out which market-place they want to sell their product (themselves) to. They must also figure out a way that they can do this most effectively. One of the problems is that many actors think successful marketing is simply developing your craft. They take acting classes, dance classes, singing classes, etc., and feel that if they're well trained and talented, they'll just be 'discovered.' That, quite often, is just a myth. They forget that this is a business, an industry. They leave out the part about being a businessperson."

### Buying and Selling in the Marketplace

When Bohlen refers to "the marketplace," she is referring to the commercial world, the soap world, TV, and stage worlds. "Actors can get further faster in their careers if they specify which market they want to go to. Within our industry, there are casting directors and agents that only work in commercials. There are casting directors and agents that just work in stage, TV, and film. If you can specify where you think you can break in the easiest, you can identify those people whom you need to sell to. For instance, if you decide that you're a good commercial type, you step into 'research and devel-opment,'" says Bohlen. You watch and study commercials. You make sure that your product identifies with that commercial. The actor's job is to find an effective way to be "identified with that market."

### How Nabisco Marketed the Oreo Cookie

To demonstrate the actor's dilemma, Bohlen uses the example of how Nabisco marketed the Oreo cookie. "They took this newly created Oreo cookie to an advertising agency. Within an advertising agency, there are three major divisions. First of all, there's research and development. In research and development, they study the product (the Oreo cookie) and identify all of the product's weaknesses and flaws. Then they develop the product until it becomes better.

"Next, the Oreo cookie goes to the marketing division. The marketing division takes the cookie just as it is. They go out to the public and tell them all the wonderful things about it, its strengths. It's the marketing division's job to sell the cookie.

"The third division, the production department, keeps producing the cookie.

"An actor has to become all three of those divisions for himself, since the actor is the product he's trying to sell. However, having the ability to stand back and become your own research and development department, your own marketing department, and your own product department is sometimes very difficult for actors."

### The Buy/Sell Line

Bohlen says that "in any business, there is a buy/sell line. In show business, agents, managers, and actors are all on the sell side. Casting directors, producers, and writers are all on the buying side of the line. What actors tend to do is keep trying to sell to people on their own side of the buy/sell line. They keep trying to sell to the agents and the managers."

Bohlen strongly advises against that. "Actors should learn to become their own research and development division, their own marketing division, and their own product division. They should sell directly to the producers, the directors, the casting directors, and the writers. Work from the top down."

### Defining Your Type

According to Lee K. Bohlen, "Actors tend to stay in the place where casting directors and agents identify them. They are categorized as young mom, young leading man, business exec, etc. We all have qualities that are beneath these surface labels.

"For example, think about Jack Nicholson. You can describe all the roles that he's played, but there's one thing that he brings to everything he does. That one thing is his 'real type.' In Nicholson's case, that real type can be described as 'dangerous and violent.' It's something you see in all of his work. It's not something that he does or has to do. He brings these qualities to everything that he plays."

When an actor can identify his real type (the type that he is even when standing still), then he can really begin his self-marketing campaign. Starting with his mailing campaign, all his future marketing should always reflect who he is. Agents specifically need to know who actors really are, type-wise. The clearer the actor is about his type, the easier it will be for the agent to know exactly what to send him out on.

When you're first breaking into the business, you'll move further and faster if you can hone in on your biggest strength. Sally Field realized this early in her career by playing roles like the Flying Nun and Gidget. She sold that one thing—innocence and lovability—completely. Meg Ryan's charm is another example. She can stand still and she's charming and you love her.

### Finding Your Type in Television Commercials

Karen Kayser, a former commercial casting director, feels that "there is a certain way in which you are perceived through the television set. This perception is often different from how you (the actor) perceive yourself." She teaches seminars that bring "actors to the mindset of the viewer."

Kayser explains: "In trying to be all things to all people, actors make their biggest mistake. They come across as smiling, one-dimensional, bland beings with no personality. In the first second of a commercial, if the viewer is not taken by the commercial, that viewer will move on to another channel.

"There has been a major shift in the advertising business to find actors who have more definition, more personality," says Kayser. "In previous years they wanted generic types; not anymore. You must find out who you are in front of the camera. The camera takes a two-dimensional picture of you, re-creating it through the TV monitor, and this is the image that the viewer gets. How you are perceived by people is a major factor in commercials. How do you see me? Actors need an outside source to give them feedback as to how they're being perceived. We are all stuck in our own mindset about ourselves. Putting yourself on videotape and then looking at the tape is one way to step outside of yourself, but even that is somewhat limited. I try to help people discover how they are being perceived visually. Commercials are not about your inner soul. They're about how you are visually perceived and whether you'll be believable as the mailman, or the librarian, etc. Wardrobe, hairstyles, makeup, are all part of the believability factor."

### An Image Consultant

Once you've honed in on your specific type and know which marketplace you're interested in pursuing, you may want to seek out an image consultant to assist you in wardrobe, hairstyle, etc. Generally, image consultants' fees vary from $300 to $750.

After several in-depth discussions with a client, the image consultant helps the client to present himself in the most suitable way for his specific type. By going through the client's present wardrobe, the image consultant eliminates clothes that are not the correct style for the specific image that the actor is trying to sell. The image consultant will go clothes shopping with the actor to help him find the most appropriate wardrobe for his new look. She'll help the actor with the best makeup and hairstyles. Don't think image consultants are just for women. Many men have found working with an image consultant to be a rewarding and profitable experience.

Laurie Krauz, a successful image consultant, feels that her role is like that of a teacher. "I give my clients information about their body types and about how to translate that information into merchandise that they find in the marketplace. Essentially, they're trying to marry three things: their body types, things they find in the marketplace, and what they do on a daily basis.

"Actors approach the industry with a belief that the art and the art alone ought to be able to get them cast. Unfortunately, we work in an industry where you can't get to the art before the facade is taken in. Decisions are made about who and what you are as a performer based on what you look like the moment you walk in the door. The first thing I say to an actor at an interview is that he needs to view himself as a can of soup on a shelf in a supermarket.

He needs to get his team of advisers together (himself) to answer a few very important questions. What is the soup? What is the flavor of the soup? What kind of packaging will best reflect that flavor? We assume that the flavor is good. That is not what the packaging is about. We have to somehow attract the people walking down the grocery aisle to pick our can of soup off the shelf.

"If you take Katharine Hepburn on one end of the continuum and Marilyn Monroe on the other end, you'll notice that one is very angular and one is very soft and curvy. These are two very different body types—the extremes, you might say. What I try to help actors do is find where they are on this continuum. Really, what we're doing is looking at bone structure. The world views us in a certain way because of the way we look. And because the world looks at you a certain way, you develop a certain personality. The Napoleonic complex grew out of the way the man looked—short.

"With actors, type is all physical, it's all body line. The actor playing Dracula is not someone short and delicately boned. Basically, people who are shorter, more curved, or, in the case of men, more triangular-torsoed are the softer body types. We generally relate to them as softer, more delicate, more romantic. That's how they're usually cast, in the less aggressive sort of roles. Generally speaking, the more angular people are cast in the more dangerous kind of roles. It's almost like we are all in agreement about what type is, and the psychology of the impact of bone structure.

"It's important for the actors to come up with the best type for themselves—a type that they feel is totally them, so that they can embody it with every inch of their skin.

"I always ask actors to list three roles that they'd be right for in the medium that they've chosen.

"Once we decide on what 'flavor of soup' you are, we can find the specifics. What colors will represent that? What kinds of shapes? Do I wear pants or do I wear a skirt? If I'm a man, do I wear a suit, or is that too fancy for me?

"Actors must always maintain a degree of professionalism in how they look. Hair combed, shoes not scuffed, etc. It's all part of the package, their presentation of who they are."

# Getting and Preparing for Interviews and Auditions

**T**wo things that almost every actor must constantly do in the entertainment industry are go to interviews (sometimes called "taking meetings" in Los Angeles) and go to auditions. Many actors find interviews and auditions everything from challenging to almost unbearable. There are those few fortunate actors who love interviews and find auditioning to be "just another wonderful opportunity to perform." Good for them—they're the lucky few.

## What Is an Interview?

An interview is a meeting with a casting director, director, producer, or agent. It's an opportunity for that person to get to know you. It's very rare that an actor is cast just from an interview, but it does happen (more in England than here). Some casting directors schedule general interviews on a regular basis.

## Meeting Agents

Perhaps the best way to get an interview with an agent is through a recommendation by a casting director who knows your work. Show business is a business of networking and making contacts. Casting directors are in daily contact with agents. Agents want to maintain solid relationships with the casting directors they work with. They trust casting directors' referrals, and if you can get one, you should easily be able to get an interview with the agent. Obviously, you should know the casting director well enough to ask for this favor. Hopefully you've booked a job through her agency, or at least had some callbacks. When asking for the casting director's help, be professional and courteous, but above all, try not to seem too desperate. A casting director's name and reputation go along with every referral.

Another way to meet agents is through actors you know. Actors whom you've worked with in shows, whom you've taken classes with, can easily introduce you to their agents. Make sure that the actor whose agent you'd like to meet believes in you. Perhaps he's complimented your work in the past. It helps if the actor and you are friends. I realize that it may feel a bit awkward to ask for his help, but unless you at least ask for his help, you'll never know. If the actor agrees, ask what he feels would be the best way for you to make contact with the agent. Would he feel comfortable calling his agent on your behalf? Or should you call his agent and use his name? Or (least preferably) should you send a picture and resume and include his name in your cover letter? If, for whatever reason, he seems uncomfortable doing this for you and refuses, don't make a big deal about it. It may have something to do with his own insecurities and nothing to do with his assessment of your talent. Just let it go, and try to get an agent another way.

Networking facilities offer agent/actor introductions and auditions for a small fee. For about $35 you get to meet with the agent that you've selected from the networking facility brochure. Most of the time agents want to see you perform a short monologue. Some agents require you to do a cold reading scene with another actor. And finally, commercial agents will give you commercial copy to read. You are not guaranteed anything from this arrangement other than the opportunity to meet with the agent.

### Mass and Targeted Mailings

Sending out unsolicited pictures and resumes to agents is one way to meet them. They may see something in your photo that interests them and call you in for a general interview. Not to discourage you, but be aware that most agents receive hundreds of photos each week.

### Making the Rounds

Years ago, actors could make the rounds of agents' offices and leave their photo and resumes with the receptionists. Since 9/11, many offices have installed security intercoms; you won't get in unless you are buzzed in. Actors are asked to either leave their photos in a basket outside the door or slip them under the door. But every once in a while, you may luck out and gain entrance and meet the agent.

Another way to meet agents is simply by calling them on the phone. But before lifting that receiver:

- Make sure you're in a good mood and feeling positive.
- Be prepared to be businesslike, direct, and brief.
- Take a breath, dial . . . and go for it!
- Understand that if you don't get past the receptionist, it's nothing personal, and it shouldn't be taken as a rejection.

### You Get the Interview: What Are You So Afraid Of?

That casting director has agreed to meet with you for an interview. Hurrah! Many actors, however, become filled with fear and trepidation as the day of the interview draws near. Why? They worry because they don't know what will happen at the interview and fear the worst. They ask questions like, What will she be like? Will she like me? What should I talk about? What shouldn't I say? What should I wear? Should I dress upscale or be more casual?

The uncertainty can terrorize you. The best way to combat this fear is to find out everything you can about the person you're going to meet and the office that you're going to. The solution to your fear is simple: prepare.

## Preparing for the General Interview: First the Facts

Find out as much as you can about the person you're going to meet. If it's an agent, try to find out who some of the agency's clients are, how long the agency has been in the business, what type of reputation it has, if it accepts videotapes, if it has offices on both coasts, what it's franchised in (theater, TV, film, commercials)—everything. Ask around, network, and ask your friends.

If it's a casting director, find out what she's cast in the past, what she's presently casting, and what she's slated to cast in the future. Find out how long the office has been in existence. Does it have offices on both coasts? What type of reputation does it have? Again, research, network, and call your friends. The more you can find out about the person who will be interviewing you, the more comfortable you'll feel. That knowledge will be helpful in alleviating your fears.

### Improvising the Interview

Once you have all the information you can find, the next step is to imagine the situation. When you think about it, most interviews, no matter what they're about, have a certain commonality. They begin when you enter the door; you say hello, you sit down, you talk, you say goodbye; and then you leave. In addition, in some interviews, you're asked to perform a prepared monologue or read some cold copy or sing a prepared song. That's about all that's going to happen. There shouldn't be too many other surprises.

While at home, improvise what you'll say. I use the word "improvise" because the last thing you want is to sound like some kind of machine spewing out memorized facts and information about yourself. Don't rehearse a memorized script—improvise.

You can be assured that interviewers will ask certain basic questions such as, So what have you been up to? and, Tell me about yourself. After looking at your resume for a moment, they may start chatting with you about a theater that you've mentioned or a director they're familiar with. This is not a quiz—don't get uptight. Prepare in advance by being very familiar with everything on your resume. While improvising at home, create imaginary conversations about items on your resume. Try to be positive in everything that you say.

Even in the case of those horrible professional experiences that you may have had, give them a positive spin. Nobody wants to hear an actor whining or complaining at an interview.

One of the great residuals of doing all this preparation before the interview is the feeling of confidence you'll have when you actually go in for the interview. You know that you've prepared to the best of your ability. And even though you still may be a little nervous, you'll be a lot more confident.

### Types of Interviews and How to Prepare for Them

There are several types of interviews for which you may be called in. I'll briefly explain what some of them are and how you can best prepare for them.

First, there's a commercial interview. Sometimes, rather than having an audition for a TV commercial, casting directors will have a commercial interview instead. The best way to prepare for this is to find out as much information as you can about the product and the specific commercial you're up for. Ask your agent to fill you in on what he knows. If you feel that what he knows isn't sufficient, then politely, professionally call the production office. Ask questions such as, Will this be a comedic commercial? and, Will it be scripted? Find out as much as you can. Whatever you learn will be helpful. Unfortunately, many times the agent won't be able to tell you too much. The best you can do is try.

Next, there's the theatrical interview. This is when you're auditioning for a play to be performed in a theater. The more you know about the particular play (not just your role or the scenes you're in), the better. Again, ask your agent specific questions about the play and the character for which you'll be auditioning. If the play is published, get a copy. If it isn't, call the casting office, and politely ask if you could come by and get a copy to read in advance. If not, could you at least come in earlier the day of your interview to read it? Find out as much as you can about the director and producer for whom you'll be auditioning. What other plays have they done? What are their backgrounds? Knowing as much as you can about them can be fodder for a good conversation when you meet with them at the interview.

Once you have some information about the play and the character, it's always wise to dress accordingly. In some situations (period dramas, historical plays), actors have made the mistake of costuming themselves. That is, rather than dressing in a manner that suggests the appropriate wardrobe, they'll rent the actual costume for that period. Aside from perhaps looking somewhat foolish, you may come across as being too desperate. *Suggesting* the wardrobe is all you need to do.

In the case of soap opera or episodic TV interviews, find out as much as you can about the show. If you're familiar with the show, don't hesitate to tell the interviewer how much you've enjoyed watching the show (and specifically tell them why).

For a movie interview, see if you can read the script in advance (more likely than not, you won't be able to). Once again, make sure that you get as much information from your agent as possible about the movie (and specifically your character).

### What Is an Audition?

For some actors, auditioning is an unpleasant, frightening experience.

Simply put, auditions are an opportunity for you to "show them what you got." You may be asked to perform material that you've prepared, such as a monologue or a scene, or you may read from a script for a director, producer, casting director, or agent.

In the case of reading from the script, you'll either be given the material in advance or right before the audition (a cold reading).

### How to Get an Audition

Aside from getting an audition through an agent, the same ways mentioned for interviews apply—that is, through personal connections, by writing, or by phoning. You may also find out about them on the bulletin boards at Actors Equity, SAG (Screen Actors Guild), or AFTRA (American Federation of Television and Radio Artists). Sometimes a friend will give you a tip about a specific audition that you can follow up on. And then there's always the trade papers that list auditions, such as *Back Stage* and *Variety*.

### Preparing for the Audition

Many of the solutions to your fears for auditions are similar to the ones I discussed in the section on interviews. Once again, the more you know about the play, the style of the play, the playwright, the character, the people who are auditioning you (the casting director, the director, the producer), and even the room in which you'll be auditioning, the better.

If it's to be a cold reading, practice your cold-reading skills at home. If the audition is to take place on a large theater stage, be prepared to project your voice and energy. If it's for a movie or TV, be prepared to be more intimate, to make your movements more subtle.

If you've been asked to bring in a prepared monologue, make sure you know it cold. Learning a new monologue right before an important audition will only add to your tension. You should have a variety of monologues prepared well in advance for all types of auditions. When you start to feel that the monologues you've been doing are stale, make sure you replace them immediately with new ones.

Preparing yourself emotionally for auditions (especially the bigger, more important ones) is a bit trickier. Certainly, you should practice relaxation and positive-thinking techniques prior to all auditions. Remember, having "nerves" isn't a bad thing if the energy is channeled directly into the audition. Each actor must find his own way of coping with the stress and pressure of auditioning. Keep in mind that the auditors really do want you to be good. The better your work, the easier their job will be. They are not the enemy. Many actors try approaching auditions with the mindset that they already have the job, and now they're just performing it. Confidence is the key. Any way you can create it in yourself for the audition is the best way.

# Videotapes

**M**ore and more casting directors and agents are now accepting videotapes from actors to see their work. One of the first questions many Los Angeles talent agents ask of prospective actor clients is, Do you have a reel? It's become almost as important (particularly in Los Angeles) as having a picture and resume. Unlike the picture and resume, however, which can be sent to practically anyone, actors should not send out their reels unsolicited.

This six- to seven-minute sampling of an actor's work can give a casting director or agent an initial idea of who the actor is, indicate how he or she looks on screen, and suggest type and range. Certainly it's not fair to say that all the actor's skills will be evident. Videotapes are made up of clips from jobs that the actor previously booked. In most cases, the emphasis was not on showcasing the actor's talent as much as moving the teleplay along, or, in many cases, showcasing the show's star. Hopefully the actor will be able to find a few moments from these taped jobs that will show at least some degree of his or her talent. Actors ask, What if I have no clips? If I've not yet done any professional work, should I make up a demo tape of monologues and staged scenes? The answer to that question depends on who you ask. Some agents and casting directors feel that it's a waste of time to make up these "homegrown" reels. Others feel that it does have some value, but only if it's very well done (which could be quite expensive) and very thought out.

### Creating Your Reel

In creating your reel, select the best sample clips from any speaking roles you've had on soap operas, films, episodic work, and any on-camera commercial work. If you don't have a copy of a particular show in which you appeared, you should contact the show's production office as soon as possible to see if it can provide you with a copy of your scene. You can get copies of TV commercials you've worked on from the ad agency (once it's been aired).

When editing material for your reel, you should find a professional, well-recommended videotape editing company. Amateur work usually looks like amateur work. It's not worth shortchanging your career just to save a few dollars. Go for the pro.

After you select the best six to seven minutes of your material, the editing studio will transfer it to a three-quarter-inch professional-quality tape. From that tape, they'll make your three-quarter-inch "master," and from that master, you'll be making all the half-inch videocassettes to be handed out to casting directors and agents.

Videotape editing can be very expensive. Generally, it will run from $250 to $500. The better prepared you are before you walk into the studio, the more you'll save in the end. All of your artistic decisions regarding the tape should be made well in advance. One way to prepare is to use a stopwatch to know exactly how much time each segment runs and figure out where you'd like it placed on the reel. Be open, however, to any suggestions that the video editor makes.

### What Should Go on Your Reel?

- Start with your name and any contact information. Some actors follow that section with a headshot.
- Select scenes that feature your character. Many times, you're hired to perform in scenes where your character is supportive

of the lead (and therefore receives little camera time). Whichever scene you choose, make sure that there are at least a few good shots of you.

- Select scenes that show you in a relationship. Quite often, how well you act is judged by how honestly you *react*.
- Try to show range of character and variety of type on your reel. The more versatile you can show them you are, the more future work possibilities there will be.
- Always keep your reel updated. You should be revising it periodically, especially if you get a great scene that show-cases your talent.
- Many actors end their reels by repeating the opening cred-its—name, headshot, and contact information.
- Something else to keep in mind: the people viewing your reel see hundreds of them. If possible, try to entertain them.

### A Reel for the Neophyte

Suppose you haven't done any professional work yet. As I men-tioned earlier, the industry is divided as to whether a homegrown reel is of any value. If you do decide to make one and plan on submitting it to specific casting directors or agents, I advise that you let them know beforehand that it's made up of staged work. Give them the option as to whether or not they'd like to see it. Don't surprise them.

When shooting your own material, consider the following:

- It's always better to select material from something that you've previously worked on. This is not the time to try out new material. Choose something from a production you once worked on, something you've developed in acting class or with your coach, or even some original material (if you hon-estly feel it's good enough).
- Try to keep your selections contemporary. Classical styles tend to look a bit stagey on camera, and unless performed with tremendous flair, can make you look like a ham.
- Try to choose material that is physically contained, shows some range, and shows you at your best. Select roles that are

within your age range and that you could conceivably be cast in. This is not a time to "stretch."

- All aspects of the production (lighting, sound, makeup, wardrobe, etc.) should be worked out prior to the day of the shoot.

### Should I Include Taped Segments from Live Performances?

Again, the answer is, it depends. Generally, these tapings emphasize the play or production, not the actor. Also, you don't usually get the close-ups that you can get in film and TV. Your voice quality may not be too good. And finally, the quality of these videotapes is usually a bit more grainy. When transferred to a reel, they lose even more clarity, sometimes making the picture seem slightly blurry or muddy. It's up to you. Remember, you can always change your mind in the studio if you discover that it's not the quality that you want on your reel.

### Who to Send Your Reel To

All right—you finally have the reel that you feel represents your talent. But then you ask, Who do I send it to? As I mentioned earlier, unlike a picture and resume (which can be sent to practically anyone in the industry), you must target where you send your reel. First of all, only send it to those people who have expressed interest in seeing it. Next, buy a copy of the *Ross Report* (and other casting books). Agents and casting directors are usually very clear as to whether they accept unsolicited videotapes. If it says "don't send unsolicited videotapes"—don't!

### Tips for Keeping Track of Your Tapes

Here are some things to keep in mind when sending out your videotapes.

- Make sure they always have your name and your address on them. That means on the tapes as well as on the boxes they're in. Many actors also glue a picture postcard to their videotapes.
- Keep a log of where all material has been sent. Include the names, addresses, and dates of material sent and when it was

returned to you. Material will only be returned if you include a self-addressed, stamped envelope.

• After a few weeks, if you haven't heard from the agents or casting directors, give them a call and politely inquire as to whether they've had a chance to see your material yet.

# Interviews with Videographers and Video Editors

In this chapter, I've interviewed several videographers and video editors. Videographers shoot your performances (scenes and monologues) live in their studios. Video editors edit pre-existing material (work from jobs you've done previously). Once again, I strongly suggest that you only have your reel done professionally.

BEN BRYANT (**BB**) is a freelance video editor. Most of the work he's done is editing preexisting footage (commercials, movies, segments from TV shows, soap operas). He's been a freelance producer for about twenty years. Bryant has produced about eight hundred to nine hundred commercials in the last fifteen years. He's done everything from McDonald's to Miller beer. He has been doing freelance editing for actors for about five years.

JONATHAN PERRY (**JP**) at Video Portfolio Productions has done most of his work over the years editing actors' reels, helping them select and organize material, and giving their reels a professional and high-quality look. Video Portfolio Productions has been in business for fifteen years.

JOANNA (**JE**) at Jan's Video Editing. Jan Natarno began this company in the late 1970s. He was one of the first people to tape shows off the air so that actors could get copies. He started a library of taped soaps and primetime shows that today is quite extensive. Jan's is one of the oldest places in Hollywood for video editing. Joanna now runs Jan's and works closely with actors in selecting and organizing material for their reels.

---

**What general suggestions and advice do you have for actors before making their videotapes?**

**BB**: First of all, hire a professional videographer to record your work. Before booking anyone, always look at a demo reel. Amateur videos generally look like amateur videos. The problem with shooting it yourself with a home video camera is technical (incorrectly framing a shot, footage severely over- or underexposed, focus jumping all over the place).

When selecting segments from work you've previously done, make sure that *you* are the highlight of the segment, not the other actors. This is your showcase, not anyone else's. If you can get the production copy, don't tape it yourself from TV. The quality is generally inferior. Don't do too much fancy stuff, just brief intros to each segment.

As far as us shooting work in the studio, it should be very short (monologues about a minute to a minute and a half long). You want to be as prepared as possible. If you're doing a scene, make sure the other actor is as prepped as you are. A scene shouldn't be more than a couple of minutes. Keep the background simple and nonspecific (e.g., a black backdrop or seamless photographic paper). Be sure you're well lit. The only thing we should be focused on is you and your performance.

Remember, the purpose of the demo tape is to show as much range as you can in as short a time as possible. Casting directors can tell within fifteen or twenty seconds whether or not you have what they're looking for. You can decide what they watch or they can decide what they watch.

Also, when hiring a videographer to shoot your live performance in a play, make sure that he is adept with lighting or sound; neither of these things can be fixed in an editing studio. When shooting live performances, generally the videographer is shooting from the back of the house. The camera with a built-in mike can hardly pick up the actor's voice. The result will be a poor-quality sound level. Also, you'll get a lot of room tone and you may even hear the camera motor hum. The videographer should use a wireless radio mike or an omnidirectional mike for scenes with several actors in them.

**JP**: You should put a lot of thought as to what goes on your reel and in which order. If you don't have too much good work, then maybe it would be better to wait until you do. I've seen too many actors put together a sloppy reel of work that doesn't really feature them. It's a waste of time and money. Also, shorter is better unless you've got a drop-dead dramatic scene.

If you want us to shoot your work while you're performing in a show in the theater, we have to work closely with the lighting designer to get the best quality. We can do a lot with lenses, but you must be well lit.

As to taping performed work in a studio, it generally looks cheesy. Unless you're willing to spend a lot of money, it generally doesn't look that good.

**JE**: The strongest work should come up first because you don't know how long someone will actually view the demo. Keep it as short as possible (five minutes or less). You'll get a much better quality. Casting directors are really just looking to see how well you act. Don't spend unnecessary money on special effects to jazz up your tape.

**What are the biggest mistakes actors make when they bring in their videos to be edited?**

**BB**: The classic is really trying to put too much on the reel. Also, bringing in taped scenes that don't really show them off. Another big mistake that actors make is that they want to add too many special effects to their reels. They want all this stuff at the beginning of the reel, lengthy lead-ins and fancy intros—all unnecessary. As one agent once said to me, "What are they trying to hide?" My feeling about videos is that you have the actor's name at the beginning and *bang* you get right to the material. I also feel you should have the actor's contact number at the end of the reel, not at the beginning. If the actor has the opening title, whether it's *Guiding Light* or *The Terminator*, I'll put that up and *boom*, get right to them in their scene.

**JP**: Many actors come in here and want to preserve the sense of the film (the narrative) on their reels. It can't be done—there's not enough time on your reel. You're not showcasing the film. Remember, the reel should only be five to seven minutes. Think only of your work. Get a three-quarter-inch tape from the production company (rather than a VHS) for a better quality.

Actors waste a lot of time in the editing studio. They should do all their decision-making at home, before they get to the studio; otherwise it's going to cost them.

When you shoot your monologues and scenes in a studio, here are some things to remember:

- Don't try to do things that are too elaborate.
- Don't get too caught up in props.
- Don't act as you would on the stage. Video acting, like film acting, should be honest but much smaller than on stage. Usually, I'll want to get in close with the camera. If you're too big, it won't look real.
- Don't worry too much about action. Don't do too much physical stuff.
- Don't wear bright red—it bleeds.
- An actor who has dark skin should not wear bright white shirts. All the light goes to the shirt, which makes it very hard to get your face to expose properly.
- Striped or checked patterns don't come out well on video (they shimmer).

**JE**: Many actors don't have their tapes keyed up to their scenes. We waste valuable studio time looking for their scenes. Also, many actors have no idea what they want their tapes to look like. If they have agents, they should confer with them. The agent will be shopping it.

**What should and shouldn't an actor expect from a professional videographer? What should and shouldn't an actor expect from a video editor?**

**BB**: The first questions I'm usually asked is, How much will this cost? and, How long will it take? It's impossible to answer these questions because it really depends on the material the actor has selected and how well prepared he is. I can tell you how long it *should* take to shoot a one-minute monologue. But I can't know if you fluff your lines, if you'll want it shot from nine different angles, etc. The same is true for editing someone's reel.

Some things you should look for and ask yourself when looking at the videographer's reel of studio work are:

- How does the actor look on camera?
- What do you think of the studio's lighting? Is the lighting appropriate for the scene? Is the lighting for the serious material the same as the lighting for the comedic material?
- Is the background setting distracting? You don't want to see bad shadows or inappropriate things (like the edge of somebody's desk, or a bookcase).

One thing an actor shouldn't expect is for the video editor to fix a bad performance. Many of the things we discussed (bad lighting, bad sound, etc.) can't be fixed. Also, please remember when you videotape a show from TV on your VCR, *always* record at standard speed and on a high-quality tape. The editor can't fix the tape once it's been recorded at too slow a speed. It's always good to try to get a copy right from the master. You'll get a better-quality reel. Contact the producers and see if they can get you a copy.

**JP**: Digital (computer-based) editing is becoming more and more the thing these days; we can do a lot more. But even with that, you shouldn't think that we can help you if your tape is of a poor quality. One thing I can do sometimes is edit a scene to favor your work. Actors should also expect a studio to have basic titling capabilities.

**JE**: Don't expect editors to read your mind. You must know what you want and be clear about it. Editors usually have a really good eye and can be of immense help if allowed. The scenes done in the studio usually look like a home video. We don't really recommend them. If you must do them, keep them simple and be well rehearsed.

### Companies That Make Actor Videos

Image Video NY, Inc.
(212) 594–8599
*www.ivny.tv*

Top of the Heap Designs
(212) 568–7949
*www.brucealanjohnson.com*

Ampere Productions
(888) 380–3695
*www.ampereproductions.com*

# Actor Directories

**A**ctor directories are books (and now also CD-ROMs) listing actors' names, photos, contact information, and sometimes a brief
mention of some of their more recent credits. The books are catego-
rized by types, such as leading man and woman, ingénue, younger
leading man, character/comedienne female, character/comedian
male, child female, and child male. Casting directors refer to these
books quite often when casting different projects.

### The Academy Players Directory

This directory, known as the industry's "casting bible," has been in
existence since 1937. About 20,000 actors are listed each year. It's
used more often on the West Coast, but also lists actors living on the
East Coast. The directory lists your name, physical characteristics,
representation, specific casting categories, union affiliations, special
skills, and professional credits. *The Academy Players Directory* request
that you submit the following:

- A completed submission form. To receive a form you can
  request one from: *The Academy Players Directory*, 8949

Wilshire Blvd., Beverly Hills, CA 90211–1972, (310) 247–3058

• An eight-by-ten headshot.


### The Link (The Academy Players Directory Online)

In July 1996, the Academy and Breakdown Services, Ltd., which supplies the entertainment industry with daily information about available acting roles, forged an alliance to develop new ways for agents and casting directors to do their jobs, utilizing rapidly changing technological tools. The resulting electronic system, The Link, streamlines the photo submission process between talent agents and casting directors. Under the new system, Breakdown Services electronically transmits its daily breakdowns of available acting roles to its clients. Using the photos and resumes from *The Academy Players Directory*, those agents may then electronically transmit to casting directors the names of talent they would like to see considered for the roles described in the breakdowns. As the incoming e-mail-like transmission links with the casting director's computer, he or she will find the submitted actor's photo and resume. In the past, this process required the physical delivery of paper and photos, using messengers and taking several hours. This free service provided by *The Academy Players Directory* (to all actors listed in the directory) allows agents to submit actors to casting directors electronically.


### Showfax's Actors Access

For more than thirty years, having pioneered the concept of breakdowns, Breakdown Services has worked with casting directors, talent representatives, and managers. One of their services is to develop the casting requirements for projects, including the specific roles and descriptions that casting directors request. Similarly, in 1993, Showfax created the means for actors to receive their sides and audition material conveniently and directly via fax or by download via the Internet. Actors Access was subsequently introduced, providing actors with a submission window to the breakdowns that casting has authorized and posted for Actors Access.

Anyone can check out the breakdowns on Showfax's site. There is never a charge to read the breakdowns posted on Actors Access. If you want to submit your information to casting electronically, you may register on the site. You will be sent an e-mail containing your new system password, at which point you can enter your profile and resume and upload your photos.

Subscribers to Showfax service can utilize the electronic submission service without additional charge or increased pricing plans. Membership in Showfax is all-inclusive. Non-members can also submit electronically for a nominal processing charge. Any qualified actor can submit hard copy on his own via Actors Access Breakdowns, though some casting directors prefer the electronic submissions.

Any registered Actors Access user can also freely create, maintain, update, and e-mail his resume and choice of headshot. Members will be part of a searchable database for casting director use.

For more information on Actors Access, call (212) 869–2003, or visit the Web site, *www.actorsaccess.com.*

# Promoting Your
# Career on the Internet

In the not-too-distant future, the Internet may become a great source of casting opportunities for actors. At present, however, even though the technology is available, all the kinks of online casting have yet to be worked out. My advice to actors who are thinking of listing themselves with some of the many fee-charging casting services is to hold off until you've carefully researched their validity. One thing you'll soon discover is that quite a few of these companies are fly-by-night, rip-off artists. That's certainly not to say that there aren't several reputable online companies offering valuable services to their actor clients.

There are certain things to look for before signing up with any online casting company:

- Find out how long the service has been in operation.
- Ask around—find out what kind of reputation the company has. (Try to ask other actors who may have dealt with them.)
- If the company charges a fee, find out exactly what you get for your money.
- Ask how many actor-clients it presently has.

- Find out how actors are contacted. If an interested director can only contact you by e- mail or through an agent and you don't have either, what's the point?
- See if any other theater Web sites validate the company's services (by listing it as a contact).
- Find out where it's located (get a mailing address), what its telephone number is, etc.
- When talking with the company, try to get a sense of how well organized it is, how legit it is, how well informed about the business its staff is, etc.
- Find out how many hits its Web site gets.

### Pros and Cons

I know of many actors who have gotten work in industrials, showcases, and low-budget independent films, or work as an extra, by e-mailing their photos to contacts made from casting and industry Web sites. In the last few years there has been an increase in online casting possibilities for actors. That being said, several of the casting directors I spoke with felt that online casting, for the most part, has limited potential. Former casting director Karen Kayser felt that at present, "they're not of much value, and most of them are a rip-off."

Several other casting directors (who didn't want to be quoted) felt similarly to Kayser, saying that "subjectivity" was one of the main components in casting, and that no online computer service could feel (yet).

Another thing to consider is that many of these online casting companies were started by computer businesspeople who are not very savvy about the entertainment industry. Younger, less experienced actors are certainly key targets for many of the companies.

On the other hand, online casting services are particularly good for networking. Meeting other actors online and sharing information is always useful.

### Some Online Suggestions

After researching many of the Web sites, I decided to list a few of them. My recommendations are based primarily on my own personal investigation, the site's reputation, and simple word of mouth. This is by no means a complete list. There are many other dependable sites.

### Playbill Online, www.playbill.com

America Online members can use the keyword "Playbill." Web surfers can go to *www.playbill.com*. Playbill describes their site as "a place where members can get information about the world of theater. They can participate in chats with artists, write them messages on the message boards, make contacts, and even find a job." This site is a large database with many interviews and articles about theater that actors will find of interest. In the Industry section, there is access to fourteen message boards and live chats, hundreds of job postings, newsletters from a variety of theater organizations, and a database of college programs. In the Multimedia section, you can browse through theater books, CD-ROMs, videos, scripts, audio clips, and theater art.

### Acting Biz, www.actingbiz.com

This sites offers valuable information about getting started in show business, how to audition well, etc.

### Internet Movie Database, www.imdb.com

This wonderful site gives you information on movies, actors, directors, and a great deal more.

### Backstage, www.backstage.com

You can get much of the information that appears in the weekly newspaper here. Backstage.com lists casting opportunities for actors. There is a fee for their online subscription.

### The Internet Theatre Database, www.theatredb.com

This is a great site to get information about a theater, a specific play, an actor, or even the title song in a musical.

### Broadway.com, www.broadway.com and www.theatre.com

This site has theater reviews and lists which plays are currently in theaters. It is a good source of up-to-date theater news.

**Breakdown Services, www.breakdownservices.com**

Breakdown Services is a vital venue for agents and casting directors who are attempting to get work for their clients. Actors are not supposed to have access to it, although over the years, many actors have figured out ways around that. Of course, nowadays, Breakdown Services has a Web site that is made specifically for actors; see the discussion of www.actorsaccess.com in chapter 11.

**Your Own Web Site**

These days, many actors have their own Web site. According to Kristine Kulage of Broadway Web Design, a company that designs actors' Web sites, "a Web site serves as an online resume easily accessible from any computer anywhere in the world. There, prospective hiring directors and agents can view an actor's resume, headshots, and career highlights, as well as a bit of his personality as represented on the site. An actor's chances of being cast for the part are increased, even if he is unable to make it to a certain city for the audition, thanks to the online resume, headshots, and even audio or video clips."

# *Networking*

**O**ne of the earliest uses of the word "network" dates back to the sixteenth century. Then, it referred to the use of fishing nets. Perhaps the best way to define the word is as "a group you know or can get to know for the purpose of sharing information." It's both a technique and a process centered on specific goals.

### What Is Networking?

Networking is basically a social activity. You purposefully develop relationships with others, acquire advice, and exchange information. The most successful type of networking is usually done in person, but the phone and mail are often good ways to maintain your contacts, especially in cities like New York and Los Angeles.

Networking is very much an assertive process. Networkers introduce themselves to others, telephone contacts that they've made on a regular basis, write notes, make dates, and basically try to always keep in touch.

The idea in networking of "using" others can be a difficult concept to accept for a lot of people. Beginning a relationship with

other people not because we like them, but because they may be useful to us, may seem manipulative and somewhat crass. But, you must
remember, networking is a two-way street. Not only do you receive
information from your contacts, but you must also always be willing
to give information when needed. The actor who simply uses people
for personal gain and information will come across as insincere,
manipulative, and untrustworthy.

In an industry like show business where there is constant job
activity, actors need to know what's happening on a day-to-day basis.
Needless to say, networking is a powerful tool for the actor.

### Where to Network

There are networking opportunities for actors almost anywhere that
people in the entertainment industry gather. You can network at casting seminars, at auditions, in classes, at the theater, while in
rehearsal for a play, at social entertainment gatherings, at theater
fund-raisers, on a movie set, or while working on a soap opera. There
are many actor support groups that offer excellent networking opportunities. If you can't find one, start one.

### Who to Network With

Almost anyone can be a source of information, from friends to
family members to people you meet at a party. The strongest contacts are usually people who work specifically in the industry.
Actors often make the mistake of only networking with other
actors. You must remember that networking is about gathering all
kinds of industry information. Networking only with actors limits
the type of information you'll receive. Writers, designers, producers, movie hairstylists, makeup people, etc., are all valid sources
for information.

### Know What You Want

Before you actively start networking, it's very important that your
career goals be clear. The more specific you are as to what you want
and how soon you plan on reaching your goal, the better your

chances of developing successful networking sources. Be realistic. Don't be too easy; challenge yourself. Setting specific goals can be very difficult in a field like show business, because there are so many contributing factors to finding work. Actors must realize, however, that they are not helpless victims whose careers are totally dependent on casting directors and agents.

### Skills Necessary to Network

Networking isn't just overhearing other people's tips and secretly storing them away for your own private use. As I've mentioned, it's a give-and-take situation that requires specific people skills. These skills include:

- **Being committed**. First and foremost, you must be willing to devote both time and energy to networking. It's a long-term, ongoing process. You must be willing to pursue and maintain relationships with your contacts. Maintaining relationships does not mean only checking in with them when you need something. The communication must be constant, on a regular basis.
- **Showing interest in (empowering) others**. An effective networker shows a genuine interest in the people she's talking to. People need to feel that they are of value. One way to empower someone is simply to listen to him. A byproduct of empowering others is that they are much more likely to help you, offer advice, and share potential casting tips.
- **Presenting yourself in a positive, attractive, and knowledgeable manner**. We're all shy to some degree. A good networker must be assertive. Try to look your best and always put your best foot forward in networking situations. Work on your confidence, especially in social situations. One thing you may want to practice at home is a very brief introduction of yourself that you can use in any and all networking situations. First impressions are very important, especially in show business. You want to come across as open, friendly, and available to make new friends.

You must be willing to share pertinent information that could be of value to others. Let's say you hear of a movie coming into town that might be looking for an extra hairstylist. One of the contacts you've made is a hairstylist. It behooves you to call that person and let her know. Sharing information is essential to networking. Be generous.

- **Knowing how to ask good questions**. Perhaps one of the strongest networking skills you must develop is the ability to ask the right questions. You must be specific, articulate, and to the point. Use questions that start with "when," "who," "where," and "what" when you need factual information.

- **Being a good listener**. Much of good networking is just plain, good listening. This means not just listening with your ears, but also with your eyes. It means being able to look at the speaker, observing his body language, and being able to see what he's really saying. You'd be amazed at how few people know how to really listen. Many actors have a tendency to be self-absorbed and are constantly worrying about what others are thinking about them. Networking is about open communication with others.

  While in conversation with someone, give the speaker feedback through such things as eye contact, a nod, a smile, or a good question in response to what has just been said.

- **Asking for help**. Whether it's asking other actors (in your network) if they know who'll be casting such-and-such a movie, or just asking another contact for some advice or an opinion, you must be willing to ask others for their assistance. Ask for what you want and try not to be shy about it. If you've developed solid networking relationships with others, asking them for help on occasion is totally appropriate (and necessary).

- **Being able to share your successes**. Keeping the people in your network informed about your achievements is a vital aspect of successful networking. Many actors feel quite comfortable complaining about the slumps in their careers, but are reticent about sharing their successes. Sharing your success doesn't mean being pompous, nor does it mean being falsely humble. Just be proud of yourself. If you auditioned for a job and got the role, share it with your network. Your sharing may be just the right impetus that another actor needs to be inspired to get out of a slump she's in.

- **Being ready and willing to follow up**. If you say you're going to do something, then do it. How often have you said to someone, "I'll give you a call" or "Let's have lunch next week," and never followed through? When it comes to successful networking, you must keep your word. Aside from showing that you're serious about the business, it also shows that you're dependable.

### Networking at Social and Business Events

When going to social or business events, you should decide beforehand what networking goals you'd like to accomplish. Know as much as you can about the event. Who will be there? What is the purpose of the event? Try to look your best. Bring a pen and pad and some business cards. If it's appropriate, bring some eight-by-tens. The basic idea at these events is not to make a lot of contacts, but, with luck, to make some strong ones (even if it's only one or two).

- **Entering the Room**. When you enter the room, stand in the doorway for a moment. This is a time to get yourself centered and see what's going on. See who's there, who you know, who you want to know. Feel the energy in the room. Is it noisy? Calm? Is there a lot of activity? For some reason, the corners of the room are usually the places where the power groups form. Decide which people you'd like to meet and then go over to them.
- **Making the Initial Contact**. Making contact for the first time is the most difficult part of networking for a lot of people. It requires being assertive. Smile, introduce yourself, make eye contact, and shake the hand of the person you've said hello to. Don't shake her hand too tensely or too passively. Just a good, warm, friendly handshake.
- **What to Say**. After saying hello and shaking hands, you can discuss the event. If you've introduced yourself to someone whose work you're familiar with, let him know. Be genuinely complimentary if you can. If it's an actor you've recently

seen in a play or movie and you enjoyed his work, let him know. Start a conversation. Ask questions, listen to what he has to say. Notice if he seems comfortable talking with you. If it's someone you feel you'd like to maintain contact with, feel free to give him your card and/or ask him for his number. Try not to spend too much time with any one person at social events. Tell him you'll give him a call, say goodbye, and circulate. You might want to jot down any pertinent information on the back of his business card when you have a chance.

- **Dealing with People You Don't Want to Talk To**. At all social events, there are always going to be people who will approach you whom, for whatever reason, you don't care to talk to. Wasting time in conversation with them is exactly that—wasting time. The secret is simply to break off the conversation with them politely with one of several phrases. You can try, "It was great meeting you, hope to see you again." Or, "I'd really like to continue talking with you, but there are so many people I promised to say hello to." Smile, say goodbye, and then quickly go over to someone else and say hello.

- **Talking to Casting Directors and Talent Agents**. With casting directors and agents, the rules at social events are a bit different. If at an event there is a casting director or agent you'd like to meet, certainly feel free to do so. It's important, however, to sense if, when you introduce yourself to her, she is open to chatting with you. If you sense she's not, don't wear out your welcome. Just say, "My name is . . . I just came over to say hi." Then subtly, politely move on.

  If you feel she is open to meeting you, you can start off by discussing the event. If you've recently seen a film that she cast, you may want to compliment her work, talk about what you liked about the project. If you want, you can talk about yourself. But don't verbalize your resume! That is, don't stand there listing everything you've been doing professionally for the last few years. That is a bore! Actors do it all the time at social events. I'm sure it comes out of nerves, but it's very unappealing. If she asks you specifically what you've been doing lately, feel free to tell her, but be succinct. Also, remember that casting directors and agents are human beings. You should relate to them with the same social respect you would anyone else. Actors who come across as blatant self-promoters, boasting about their work in this film or that, can be annoying and obnoxious. Above all, always try to present yourself as a professional. You certainly don't want to come across as negative or unlikable. Putting down a director or producer of a project on which you worked is not smart; neither is complaining. Try to be positive and open.

## The Follow-Up

Once you've made the initial contact, the follow-up is one of the most important aspects of the networking process. Maintaining communication with your contacts is vital to successful networking.

### After the Initial Contact: Actors, Directors, Designers

A day or two after the event, you should contact the actors with whom you exchanged cards (unless they call you first). The call should be friendly, letting them know how much you enjoyed meeting them. Perhaps you can suggest getting together for coffee or lunch, or going to the theater together. Always keep the focus friendly and business-oriented. If they seem receptive, make the arrangements. If they seem somewhat reluctant or offer a lot of excuses, then politely suggest that they call you when they have a chance.

Another way of maintaining contact with people you've met is to support their work. Show up at the theater when you've found out they're involved in a play or a reading. Supporting each other through their work is a strong way to develop networking circles.

If you hear of a role being cast that one of the actors in your networking group might be right for, give her a call, let her know. If you know of a show looking for a set designer and you know one, give him a call. Be giving. What goes around, comes around.

### After the Initial Contact: Casting Directors, Talent Agents

Unless they specifically suggested that you call their offices, most casting directors and talent agents prefer not to get unsolicited phone calls. A friendly note (with a picture and resume attached) telling them how nice it was meeting them at the event is always a good idea. In your note, don't forget to remind them where and when it was that you met. Also, it helps if you can refer to anything that you discussed (they may have met a lot of people that night). Make the note polite, cordial, and brief. Tell them you'd like to keep them posted about events going on in your career. Mention that you hope they'll keep you in mind for anything that they feel you're right for in the future. Keep your word; put them on your contact list and keep them posted.

Generally, the frequency and type of contact with casting directors and talent agents will be different from the way it is with most of your networking contacts. It's a bit more businesslike, less social (usually), and more specifically work-oriented.

### Sustaining Your Networks

Keeping in touch with the contacts you've made is vital to sustaining networks. How often you've met, how well you know them, how strong the contact is, whether you speak only on the phone, etc., are factors that determine how you keep in touch. Some contacts like to be very social, while others prefer only a brief phone call now and then.

### Lunches and Get-Togethers: Expanding Your Network

Some actors create networking meetings on a weekly or monthly basis to share information and to offer support to other members. Socializing is another way to develop your networks. Inviting several of your contacts for lunch or having a party is a pleasant way to meet in groups. When people meet in small social circles, they are more relaxed, more accessible. And as you invite your contacts to social gatherings, hopefully they'll invite you to theirs. As to whether you should invite casting directors and talent agents to your networking social functions, it's a hard call. It has to do with the nature of your relationships with them and the appropriateness of the occasion. Be sensitive as to how they'd feel at such an event (and how you'd feel having them there).

# Networking Facilities

**N**etworking facilities have become one of the most effective ways to meet casting directors and talent agents, both in New York and Los Angeles. The way that these companies work is that actors select the casting director or agent that they wish to meet from a list, pay a small fee (generally around $35), and have a five-minute, prearranged audition for the casting director or agent, where they will perform a monologue, read from sides, do commercial copy, or sing. Although it is stressed that there are no guarantees of employment, this is an effective way to make initial contacts.

According to Bunny Levine, the former owner of The Actors Connection, a networking facility in New York, "They are extraordinary opportunities to meet industry guests, learn about them as people, learn about their offices, and show them a bit of your work."

Casting directors and agents meet with actors at these seminars and listen to a prepared monologue, a cold reading of a scene or commercial copy, or listen to the actor sing. According to Levine, "Sometimes positive results are immediate. Occasionally actors report auditions and bookings as much as a year after meeting a guest. And sometimes a meeting is simply a foot in the door, a first meeting that should be followed up periodically with correspondence and subsequent seminars. Or, at the very least, it enables you to invite guests to your next performance, with some assurance that they'll recognize your name and face. "Levine also says that the seminars "provide great networking opportunities with fellow actors." She does stress, however, that "meeting a guest is never a guarantee of employment."

Alan Nusbaum, who owns Talent Ventures Incorporated acting schools, which have casting seminars as part of their curriculum, says his casting seminars give actors "a great opportunity to get specific feedback on their work from working professionals. The idea of getting your work critiqued directly by casting directors can be very helpful and insightful to the actor who's ready to have his work seen professionally."

### At the Seminars: What Happens?

Most of the seminars begin with a question-and-answer period with the guest for a half-hour to forty-five minutes. It's a time for the actors to get a sense of the guest, her likes, dislikes, and specifically what her office is all about. Then, after a short break, the actors perform their prepared work or do cold readings. Generally, actors are allowed three minutes to perform a monologue (or songs, or combination thereof), or six and a half minutes for a prepared scene.

Next, the casting director gives the actors feedback on what she saw. The emphasis here should be on learning, not auditioning.

Actors should not react emotionally to the casting director's criticisms. Instead, just take them in. If you're unclear about what the casting director meant, you should certainly ask for clarification. Another, less common format is one in which the guest sees the actor for a six- to ten-minute one-on-one interview (and then sees the actor's work).

One of the benefits of these seminars is that you get to see the casting directors and agents as human beings, not as some powerful, godlike entities that can make or break your career.

### Protocol and Courtesy at the Seminar

There are certain courtesies expected from actors at the seminars. According to Bunny Levine, actors should "arrive on time and stay until the end of the seminar. You'd be surprised at how much you can learn from what the guest says to the other actors, and also at how important your presence and support are to the others." Levine says that many of the guests (the casting directors or agents) resent early departures. Also, she says, "This should be an environment of support for each other, not of competitiveness. On the rare occasion that an actor does not perform to our standards, we consult and advise him or her about classes and other ways to achieve an acceptable level of performance." Try to learn from the casting director's comments on your work. As Levine says, "Don't complain. Don't explain."

### Interviews with Networking Facility Owners

Lisa Gold (**LG**) has been a singer/actress for over twenty-five years, performing in musical theater, commercials, and cabaret, and headlining on cruise ships and indie films. She is the current owner of The Actors Connection.

Alan Nusbaum (**AN**) is CEO and founder of TVI (Talent Ventures Incorporated), one of the largest acting schools, with offices in New York City and Miami, and headquarters in Los Angeles.

***

**At what point in their careers should actors begin taking casting seminars?**

**LG**: An actor should already have his marketing tools in place (i.e., professional headshot and resume) and have at least six months to a year of professional/university training and some working experience for the seminars to be most effective. True beginners should spend their money on classes and training to make sure they are at a saleable level before meeting guests.

**AN**: When they have a good foundation of the fundamentals of acting. When they feel confident about themselves and their work. And when the actor has work that he's confident about showing.

**What are the most common mistakes actors make at these seminars? How can they avoid them?**

**LG**: Unprofessional behavior is by far the biggest downfall. Proper attire, intelligent questions, and courtesy to other actors are highly valued. Also, when performing a monologue, choose material that doesn't require loud dramatics. Remember, these guests are coming in the evening after a long day of work already. Be interesting.

**AN**: They come into the seminars seeking employment instead of coming to learn from the casting director or agent. They come across as too desperate. If the actor is confident in his talent, he shouldn't have any difficulty accepting what the guest has to say, learning from the comments, and being able to utilize them. The confident actor won't be so preoccupied with making an impression.

Another mistake that actors make at these seminars is they come unprepared. They forget their pictures and resumes, or sometimes forget something as little as having the picture stapled to the resume.

**What type of prepared material should actors select for these seminars?**

**LG**: Most seminars tell you in advance what is expected for the evening. Have several short monologues available . . . contemporary and on the lighter side (see above). No Shakespeare! Have your cold-reading skills solidly in place. Connect with the other actor or casting director you are reading with. If you are a singer, bring several selections, though you will probably only do one song. Sing your forte. If you are performing commercial copy that you can choose, be careful when selecting material. Choose something that you would possibly be cast in.

**AN**: Something light and comedic that hasn't been done a hundred times before. Make the monologues contemporary. It doesn't make too much of a difference if it's comedic or dramatic, as long as you have your moment in the monologue. When you do a comic piece that makes people laugh, they tend to remember you more. With scenes, problems come up when the scene is too long, or when the actor "over-props" it and it becomes a scene about props.

**What types of mistakes do actors make when doing cold readings at these seminars?**

**LG**: A lot of actors are overly concerned about the exact words on the page. At these seminars, the writer is not present (you can worry about that at an actual audition). Connect with the other reader and really LISTEN when he is speaking. Don't just look down on the page when you're not talking. Connecting is key. Also, don't do anything in the room that wasn't rehearsed with your partner out in the hall, i.e., kissing or touching her, doing something out of the ordinary . . . It throws off your partner and you end up looking bad.

**AN**: Not listening to his partner. The actor has an agenda going. He doesn't respond to what's being given to him by the other person.

**What is considered appropriate/inappropriate behavior at these seminars between the actor and the guest?**

**LG**: Don't ask questions of the guest that are too personal like, Where do they hang out after work? During a group Q&A, don't ask questions that are related only to you personally . . . include the room. The guest's answers should benefit everyone participating. Again, if the guest is reading with you, don't touch him in any way. Appropriate distance is good. And don't yell at the guest!

**AN**: Respect the person's position. Always show up early for these seminars. The actor should not approach the casting director and ask, Are you currently looking for such-and-such? Questions that come down to—Are you going to hire me? Are you going to bring me in for this role? Are you going to represent me or freelance with me?—are not really even self-serving. They're just stupid and counterproductive.

**What factors should actors keep in mind when selecting guests?**

**LG**: If you are a newer actor with few paying credits on your resume, your best bet is to see casting directors [rather than agents] in the beginning. They often bring actors in directly for auditions. This gives you the opportunity to build your resume with paying experience and will attract a good agent in the future. Choose guests that focus on what you say you want in a career. For example, if film and television are your goals, don't see guests who cast primarily theater. Independent casting directors who do a little bit of everything are a sure bet, as they have diverse needs for various projects. Unless you are confident that you are extremely talented and have the credits on your resume to support that, don't see agents who do not freelance and only sign . . . that's tough.

**AN**: Go to a variety of casting director seminars. You can gain some value from the variety of casting directors' responses. Actors should do some research before making any selections. For instance, if the actor is just starting out and doesn't have too much experience, he might want to take a seminar with a smaller agency that could be more open to him.

# Talent Tours

**T**alent tours are junkets with groups of actors that go to specific cities (primarily Los Angeles or New York) where actors are likely to find substantial work opportunities. There they meet with and showcase their talent for casting directors and agents who work predominantly in that area. They are geared toward the actor who is of one of two minds: First, the actor who has decided to move there and wants to get all the information he can before going; or, second, the actor who is seriously considering moving, but before making the trip "cold turkey," wants something to base the move on. During these junkets, the actors get an opportunity to network with people who are players within the industry. They get to experience how the business is different in that city. Junkets go to New York City, Los Angeles, Chicago, and sometimes other cities. Some of these seminars also include meetings with local photographers and real estate agents who can help actors with housing. One thing that actors should realize is that these tours should not be thought of as a vacation.

## Interviews with Talent Tour Operators

LISA GOLD (**LG**) was an actress for more than twenty-five years. She is the current owner of The Actors Connection.

ALAN NUSSBAUM (**AN**) is the founder of TVI (Talent Ventures Incorporated).

---

### Why and when should an actor take a talent tour?

**LG**: It's a way to test the waters before diving in. A way to get a sense of what is to be expected if you do actually move there. It demystifies that market and makes it more possible for you to get a running start if you do decide to move.

**AN**: When an actor is considering moving to Los Angeles in the next twenty-four months, this is a great opportunity to check it out. He or she can see what it's like before moving out there. Travel tours also provide the actor with contacts when he or she does move out there. Aside from finding out where to live, the actors get to know different agents and casting directors and get a sense of what they expect of actors.

### What occurs on these tours on a day-to-day basis?

**LG**: In our program, which is distinct from others that are offered, the actor has a chance to have a mini-interview with each guest before he/she performs. This is where you get to show a little bit of who you are and create that all-important connection to the guest. Then the group comes together and the guest goes over exactly what his office does and answers questions. He hands out scenes and, after a short rehearsal period, you will perform and get feedback. We do a week-long trip that typically runs from 10:00 A.M. to 10:00 P.M. daily (three guests per day), with a few mornings or evenings off to explore the city. We also have a comprehensive orientation on the market, the best resource materials, places to live, day jobs, studio locations, etc. We have fifteen guests from various backgrounds: network television dramas and sitcoms, independent film casting directors, smaller studio casting directors, legit agents. And, because commercials are equal on both coasts, we spend one seminar with both a commercial agent and casting director together. Outside of that double team, we never present them on a panel; all are presented individually. Oh, and another thing . . . no monologues! (At least in L.A. It's a cold scene town.) We wrap up the week with a big completion party! Usually, over 75 percent of every group we take out ends up moving there.

**AN**: We usually do these tours five times a year. There are generally about twenty-four actors in each group (generally two groups go out there at the same time). They usually start at ten in the morning. The majority of actors stay at a hotel that we arrange for them, which is only a mile from our studio in Los Angeles. There are five or six sessions a day. Each session begins with a question-and-answer period where the actors can learn about the casting director, her office, and what she casts. Then, the casting director hands out scenes and works with each actor individually. Next, the actors are critiqued and get feedback on their work.

**What should/shouldn't an actor expect from these tours?**

**LG**: Don't expect to be in that market for a week, meet guests, and immediately book work. The reason to do the trip is for the experience of what working and auditioning would be like if you actually moved there. Many people have been called for auditions and bookings while there, but it is not to be expected. The point of doing the trip is to determine for yourself whether you can commit to the move and have a career. You will be clear at the end of our trip whether to go or not to go!

**AN**: You shouldn't expect to be signed on the spot. If you're what they're looking for, they have your resume. You have to learn to be patient. You can get a point of view on your work that might vary a bit from the New York casting directors. The needs in Los Angeles are different than in New York. Being a New York actor with substantial theater credits is always a plus out there.

**What do actors need to prepare for these tours?**

**LG**: Again, have all of your marketing tools in order. Be ready for anything and everything. Be a sponge and learn everything you can so that you can make an informed decision on whether to move. You can't expect to go for a week, come home, and wait for the phone to ring. Isn't it hard enough getting work where you *do* live? You'll need to actually spend time in the community where you choose to have your career. After you're established a bit, you might be able to do the bicoastal thing. Get lots of rest and prepare yourself for an experience of a lifetime!

**AN**: Two monologues, casual clothing, lots of pictures and resumes, and that's about it.

# *Talent Agents*

**T**alent agents do not get you jobs. Despite what many actors believe, only you can get yourself an acting job (usually through an audition). Agents may recommend you for a job. They submit your picture and resume to casting directors. They can set up appointments, interviews, and auditions for you. And, occasionally, they can give you some career guidance.

The talent agent is the seller in the equation, the casting director is the buyer, and you, the actor, are the product. Simplistic, perhaps, but—show business is a business.

Most agents are franchised (licensed) by all of the actors' unions (Actors Equity Association, SAG, and AFTRA). In Los Angeles, many agents don't have Actors Equity franchising for theater and quite often it is not a medium that they choose to work in. It is to your advantage as an actor to work with franchised agents only. By law, they must follow certain ethical and professional standards. You must do this, by the way, even if you yourself are not a member of any of the three unions that franchise agents. Union actors can only work with agents that are franchised in their particular affiliations.

### Commissions

Talent agents receive a 10 percent commission for their services. The 10 percent commission that they are entitled to is paid only after you are paid, never before. There are some stories of unscrupulous agents who ask for their commissions in advance. This is not the way it works.

### Freelance versus Signed

There are two ways an actor can work with an agent: freelance or signed. When an actor freelances with one agency, he has the right to freelance with other agencies. That is, there is no exclusivity to the professional commitment; other agents may also send him out on auditions.

A "signed client agreement" occurs when an agency and an actor have agreed to work exclusively with each other (either in a particular area, or in all three areas). The actor cannot freelance with any other agency in the field(s) that the contract covers.

There are agencies that handle only freelance clients, and there are signed-client-only agencies. A third type of agency handles both freelance and signed clients. In this case, the agencies try to find work for their signed clients first. Beneath the signed clients on the totem pole are the freelance clients, whom the agent calls when none of his signed clients fit the bill for a particular job.

### When to Seek Representation

Jonn Wasser, one of the talent agents that I interviewed for this book, said, "Agents are looking for actors who aren't looking for agents. Agents are looking for actors that are going places." Perhaps one of the biggest turnoffs to most talent agents is meeting desperate actors who believe that they can't have any kind of a career without an agent. That desperation permeates their interviews and sometimes their work. Generally, in Los Angeles, you need representation to get most work.

Actors living and working in New York City, however, can fend for themselves without an agent.

Before seeking representation, make sure that you're really ready. Being ready means having enough training under your belt. You must feel confident about yourself and your talent. You must be able to present yourself as personable and professional. The agent must believe in you and must feel passionate about your talent.

Experience is another factor that agents consider before signing an actor. The more professional theater, film, and television experience you have, the better.

If you're just out of school, try to get into some acting showcases, some independent and student films. Do some extra work and under-five work on soaps. Get your face seen; build up your resume.

For those actors who are more experienced (and have signed with talent agents previously), the questions for both the actor and the prospective agent are, What can the agent do to move the actor's career to the next level? and, What can be done that hasn't been done previously?

Both experienced and inexperienced actors need to research the agents they're interested in. You might want to know which actors they work with (their client lists). You may be too similar to some of their existing clients. Are they the right-sized agency for you? They could be too big (you could get lost in the shuffle) or not big enough (when you're better connected with casting directors than they are).

It's also important to find out about the other agents at the agency with which you are considering working. How long have they been with this agency? What are their backgrounds? Would you feel confident with them representing you, negotiating for you? Do they see you the way you see yourself (type- and talent-wise)?

# Interviews with Talent Agents

**M**ARTIN GAGE (**MG**), of the Martin Gage Agency in Los Angeles, handles talent for film, TV, and theater. He has been an agent for thirty-nine years. His agency opened its New York City office in 1973 and its West Coast office in 1975. He presently represents or has represented Robert Pastorelli, Geraldine Page, Kim Basinger, Woody Harrelson, and Bernadette Peters.

JONN WASSER (**JW**) is an agent with Atlas Talent. Prior to creating Atlas Talent, he was with the Don Buchwald Agency for eight years. Before that, he was head of the Corporate Sponsorship Program at Radio City Music Hall.

MARK REDANTY (**MR**), of Bauman Hiller and Associates' New York City office, has been an agent since 1984. He represents or has represented Robert Morse, Donna McKechnie, Scott Wise, and Jodi Benson.

SUSAN SMITH (**SS**) is with Susan Smith and Associates in Los Angeles. The agency has been in business for over thirty-five years.

**How would you describe your job?**

**MG**: My job is twofold: to get jobs for people and negotiate contracts, and to guide careers. Part of my job is also managerial; that is, I also do what some managers do.

**JW**: Basically, I'm a salesman. I sell talent. We're licensed by the city of New York as an employment agency. I seek out opportunities for clients, primarily now in the broadcast-promotional field. For instance, you'll hear on TV, "Coming up on Channel 4, Glen Smith talks about so-and-so." That's called a promo, which is one type of voice-over that's highly competitive but is also highly lucrative.

**MR**: My definition of an agent comes from the play *End of the World* by Arthur Kopit. In it, there's an agent who says, "An agent's function is to field offers for her clients." I try to help my clients get work, and then negotiate their contracts.

**SS**: What I do is find work for actors. Talent agencies are really employment agencies for actors. I also guide actors' careers and help with decisions in career planning.

**How and where do you find the actors you work with?**

**MG**: I find them all over. I used to find them at schools. I found Tim Robbins at UCLA. I've found a lot of actors in showcases. But I can tell you that you can see five hundred actors before you sign one. My agents go to see everything and we watch television. The advent of the videotapes has been extremely helpful for us in finding new talent.

**JW**: Referrals, showcases, voice-over tapes. Just to mention it, the voice-over tapes have to be perfect. Otherwise, it's a waste of time. We scout comedy clubs a lot.

**MR**: I interview at least one actor every day in my office. I meet many of them through referrals. Also I give seminars on "How to Get Your Career Started" at schools all around the country. I've met clients there while they're still in school. I'll go to schools such as Boston University, University of Utah, and North Carolina School of the Arts.

**SS**: In the beginning, I used to go to every basement and attic to find talent. Today, the way the agency is, it's primarily through recommendations and also at the drama schools.

**What types of things do you look for in a headshot? On a resume? On a videotape?**

**MG**: Headshots must look like the person. I'm an eye person, so I look to their eyes in their photos. We sometimes get forty photos a day. It's rare that we call in someone just from the photo, but if the face has something really extraordinary going on . . .

On the resume you want strong credits, but I'll tell you, I've taken people who have had no credits, right out of the schools. When someone lies on his resume, it's very annoying. But everyone does it. I used to do it when I was a young actor. But it doesn't pay. You get caught. When I see a credit for a show that I saw, I know whether or not they were in it. And I can easily find out. I have almost every playbill of every play I've seen since 1950, and I have notes. So I go home and check on it. Or they'll say they were directed by so-and-so, and that director's a friend of mine. A phone call later and the truth comes out. It's very simple to check on someone's credits.

The videotape and CD has become very important. When you don't know someone's work firsthand, that videotape is like gold. Basic acting skills are immediately apparent. Presence is obvious. I won't look at a poorly made tape. It must be a professional tape with professional jobs that you've done. Six minutes at most. One good scene can tell me all about you, but two or three is preferable. And it shouldn't be a scene where there are five guys sitting around a table talking, and all of a sudden you come running in with your two lines. The most important thing for an agent is that he knows what to do with you, how he can best sell you. The videotape or CD must offer him some clue. If you don't know who that actor is and what he does, then how can you sell them?

I've had actors, especially New York actors, who say, "Just take a chance and send me out." I have a reputation too. This issue is really a problem. You must know what you can do, how you can best sell the actor.

**JW**: Since I still work on a lot of on-camera commercials, all of those things apply to me. On the headshot, the personality must pop out. Obviously, good looks count first. It's like a blind date. The good-looking person will get through the door easier. On the resume misspellings turn me off. Then you know the actor doesn't consider himself a professional. I look for substantial credits unless you're twenty-two and right off the boat. The videotapes and CDs help also. Is he mesmerizing on camera? Is there something in his performance that pulls me in? Does his picture match his videotape (which many times it doesn't)?

**MR**: If I'm looking at a picture and the actor is absolutely gorgeous, naturally that'll interest me. But that's not to say that's all I look for.

On the resume: good training, good experience based upon age. Number of years in the business.

On the videotape and CD: You assume that the videotape or CD is a good representation of the actor's work, and it isn't always. Sometimes the actor has not been given the right types of opportunities. I'd rather see what the actor will choose on her own, like a monologue in which the actor is showing you what she considers to be the best of her work. Actors who have been around a while may have a volume of work on their videotapes. Young actors who haven't booked that much yet may be brilliant, but they just haven't had the opportunity. I'm a New York agent, and I'm very much into theater.

**SS**: I want the headshots to be interesting. I don't like when they're arty. I prefer darker colors in the photos. I certainly don't like "model-y" looking photos. Most of my clients are pretty well known, so in many cases, I don't have to send their photos over to the casting directors. As for the resume, I want to see good theater credits. As for a lot of episodic work on TV, don't waste all the space. Just list numerous episodes of such-and-such a show.

Never list commercials. As for the videotapes and CDs, I'd rather have one good piece than several little snippets from several shows.

## When interviewing actors, what do you look for?

**MG**: As I said, Do I know what to do with you? Do I want to do it with you? I must like you. I need to believe I'll be able to work with you, that you will be easy to work with, that you will fit into this office. Also, at the interview, it's really a waste of time to complain about your former agent and how he "done you wrong." I immediately think, If I work with this actor and it doesn't work out, will he be bad-mouthing me to the next agent?

**JW**: I look for them to run the interview. If I have to pull it out of you, it makes my job very difficult. But if I saw you in a brilliant showcase and I think you're the next Brad Pitt, I don't give a hoot if you sit there and suck your thumb. However, a lot of it is about personality. An actor can do his homework before an interview. It's one thing he can do to prepare. Find out who we represent, a little bit about me. But the bottom line is, be yourself. Don't put on any airs. Relax. As crass as this sounds, you must realize that you're a commodity, you're the product. Look around at what people are buying. Seems very basic and crude, but that's it in a nutshell. Market yourself as a product.

**MR**: I try to get the actor to relax and be himself. I need to find out if this is the kind of person I want to work with the rest of my career. I want to see if he has a sense of his ability in relation to the industry. I want to see if he knows what the industry is like. Is he a team player, someone easy to get along with?

**SS**: I look for an intelligent person. Show me a stupid person, and I'll show you a stupid actor. Tell me who you are as a human being. I can see all your credits on the resume—now tell me about you. What's important to you in life? What makes you the person that you are?

**Do you have a specific process, a way of working with the daily breakdowns?**

**MG**: I don't do much of the day-to-day anymore. I handle a lot of the selling of movie scripts in the agency. I do a small amount of the submissions. Certain casting directors are very demanding, and they have a right to be. Generally, I'll work with them personally. They also have known me for a very long time. As for the breakdowns, I always like two views on everything.

**JW**: I deal with commercial breakdowns. There might be one a day. Most of what I do is on the phone. For instance, one casting director, casting a Tide commercial for one day, might call five or six agents. They'll call, not put it in a breakdown. We'll get a call for an AT&T commercial. They'll be looking for two businessmen. One in his fifties, a CEO type, one in his thirties, a young executive. The whole process is much quicker. We'll get the call Monday, it casts Tuesday, the callbacks Thursday, and then it'll shoot the following Monday. The way I decide which actors to send is by being familiar with the types that AT&T has been using most recently in its current spots. Always be aware of the immediacy of a commercial. You have just seconds to catch the viewer's attention and belief. You've got to be right on target in your casting.

**MR**: My associate does the breakdowns first, and then he brings them in to me. Then I add or subtract anyone that I feel he may have overlooked. I tend to over-submit rather than under-submit. I'd rather have the casting director say no than not give the actor the opportunity because I didn't submit her. I submit based on age and ability, and obviously, who's most right for it. The more explicit the breakdown, the more you can do. What I don't like is when you have a breakdown that doesn't have any ages delineated. I generally use the breakdown as the main information first, and then look at the script, which I usually get later. I feel that the casting director has been discussing it with the author or with the director and has a much clearer idea of what this character is than I do based on my reading of the script.

**SS**: We work with the breakdowns but only as an adjunct to reading the script. But you can't get every single script read. Sometimes I get backed up because I also am reading books for some of my clients for future film projects. Some of my clients are now also directing. So there's a lot of reading to do. Clients like Brian Dennehy, Kathy Bates, and Greta Scacci, for instance, are involved with a lot of potential projects that I'm involved with. I try to be creative with the breakdowns. Certainly, I can't send a fifty-year-old for the role of a college student. But I send very few people for a part. If I send more than two, it's unusual. This is because I never represent any two actors who are that similar. Therefore, no conflicts.

### What do you enjoy most/least about the work you do?

**MG**: Finding someone and helping him to become a star is very gratifying. It's upsetting when you lose a client you've helped to develop. I believe it's mostly the younger kids coming up who don't understand the loyalty. They feel that by going with a larger agency, they'll be packaged better. Let me tell you something: There are really only about six actors in America you can really package. Another great part of this job is the acknowledgments. When Jane Anderson won the Emmy for the TV movie "The Confession of the Texas Cheerleader's Murder Mom" and said, "I want to thank my agent, Martin Gage," it was a great moment. When Debra Monk won the Tony and acknowledged the agency, that too was wonderful.

**JW**: Mostly, I enjoy booking talent and discovering somebody.

**MR**: What I enjoy most is saying, "You got the job." Also, being there when one of my clients is honored for the work she's done. What I enjoy least is working with casting people who are not open to meeting people they've never met before, and are not open to meeting actors who've done one area of work and aren't being considered for another. What I mean is allowing an actor who has mostly done theater to try working in film. Or that an actor who's done mostly television can also do theater. I also don't enjoy dealing with the casting director who feels that an actor who's done only musicals can't do anything else but musicals.

**SS**: What I enjoy most is my clients. What I enjoy least is the whole business. It's not a very nice place anymore. I've had a company for almost twenty-eight years and I've watched the ethics, values, taste, and creativity slowly disappear.

### What is the one thing that actors do that really ticks you off?

**MG**: Lying. Not showing up for appointments. Sometimes an actor will say, "I don't want to play this part." Sometimes I know what actors can do better than they do. I try to help them by convincing them. Some actresses decide that they only want to play beautiful. Actors have visions of themselves that are restrictive. I've changed careers. I worked with Geraldine Page at a time when her movie career was pretty much over. She wasn't a leading lady anymore. I got her the Woody Allen movie *Interiors*. She didn't want to do it. I said, "What are you, crazy?" She said, "That character's a fat, old matriarch." I convinced her to do it. God, how I loved that woman. She was a great, great actress.

**JW**: I think it's that many actors presume that it's all about them, their egos, the self-absorption. When I'll meet an actor socially and say, "Hi, how are you?" He'll tell me about his latest booking. Many actors don't look at agents as human beings, but only as a way to get more work for themselves.

**MR**: When, at an audition, an actor is asked to make an adjustment and doesn't quite succeed. Then, when walking out the door, he realizes what the director meant. Rather than turn around and ask if he can try it again, he just leaves. He has nothing to lose by asking. The worst he can hear is no. Something else that bothers me is the actor who shows up at an audition without a picture and resume, assuming that the agent already sent it in. Quite often the agent did, but the casting director hasn't opened that envelope yet. Another thing is showing up at an audition where they want you to sing and you bring only one song. They love it and ask you, What else have you got? And you're left standing there. Another thing that gets to me is actors who don't take responsibility for their careers, but put that responsibility on other people.

**SS**: An actor who calls every day and asks, "Am I up for anything?"

**What suggestions do you have for actors to: a) to help themselves promote their work and b) to make themselves known to agents?**

**MG**: Networking is very important. Do a showcase, do a play. Out here, some agents feel that booking an actor to do theater isn't profitable enough. There is a mentality out here, mostly among the younger agents at the bigger agencies, to only show big figures and to only go for the big money. I tell my actors that they should do a play at least every two years. You can learn a lot of tricks in this business. Robert Pastorelli was one of my clients. He had leads in movies, did very well. Once every year or two, at the most, he did a show at the Ensemble Studio Theater or somewhere else. Just to keep at it. That's why he was so good. Never assume that you're there.

**JW**: If you're in a good showcase, someone will come to see it. Word travels—you'd be surprised. Every actor needs to find a "rabbi" within the office to champion him or her. The rabbi is that agent in the office who will promote him or her to other agents. Anyone who has ever succeeded in this business has had a champion.

**MR**: Get out there and get into something where your work can be seen. Create a vehicle for yourself, like Chazz Palminteri and Eric Bogosian have done.

**SS**: As far as actors I don't represent go, I don't particularly want or need to know what they're doing. I'm only really interested in the clients I do represent. I'm not looking to broaden my talent base here. That's not to say if a twenty-two-year-old Robert Redford came to me, I'd turn him away. As for the clients I do have, all I want for them to know is how to walk through the door and secure the job. It's called "the art of auditioning." It's very different from being a wonderful actor. It can be taught, and actors need to learn.

**What factors go into your choice of working with one actor over another?**

**MG**: As I said earlier, How can I sell this actor? What is so unique about him or her?

**JW**: The actor's experience, what other people feel, what my gut feeling is, which actor I feel will make the most money. Who I feel will make the most money is probably the most important factor.

**MR**: Whether I think I can get him work, whether I feel I can work with him, whether I like him, whether I respect his talent.

**SS**: I must feel some passion for her talent. If I don't really believe in someone, how can I personally convince a casting director of her talent?

**If you had one piece of advice to offer actors regarding their careers or this business, what would it be?**

**MG**: (*laughing*) Be a lawyer! Twenty years ago I would have said, Be a doctor! If you're young and are very dedicated, don't give up!

**JW**: You have results or you have excuses. Anybody who's ever made it on any level has always been focused on the results.

**MR**: Study. If you were a musician, you'd be practicing every day. You want to get ahead—learn what you're doing.

**SS**: Probably, get out. You must really, really want it. Because the way that actors are treated is so revolting, you must have a tremendously tough skin to get through the process. This country does not have a tradition for respecting actors. There's only a tradition for idolizing movie stars.

**Is there anything else you'd like to suggest or comment on for a book of this nature?**

**MG**: This isn't the business I came into. It's changed tremendously. You can always tell the potential stars. The first star I ever worked with was Bernadette Peters, about thirty-five years ago. From the very first minute, I knew. You couldn't stop Bernadette. There's no way she couldn't become a star. Same thing with Woody Harrelson. And this isn't just about talent. Talent isn't what gets you a job. Talent is what keeps you working. When Kim Basinger walked into my office for the first time—I knew. I thought, I can make this one a star in about eleven minutes. And I didn't know she could act. Her presence was unbelievable.

**JW**: Actors must be prepared to be judged twenty-five hours a day. It's the hardest business in the world. You have to be able to tolerate an unhealthy amount of rejection and scrutiny. And quite often, you're not even aware of who's judging you at what time. Embrace where you're making the money now and be satisfied. But always be looking for the next step. You're always auditioning.

**MR**: Instead of beating your head against the wall trying to get an agent to take responsibility for your career, create your own career. If your career's in a slump, you need to create a spin about yourself, and I, as an agent, can't do it for you.

**SS**: I feel all actors should be trained. If you believe the assumption, and I do, that most directors aren't very good, you must be well trained so you can fall back on yourself. You must be self-reliant.

# *Personal Managers*

I contacted Gerard W. Purcell, former national president of the Conference of Personal Managers, to discuss the role of personal managers in an actor's career. He has managed such diverse talents as Maya Angelou and Al Hirt.

### What Managers Do

According to Purcell, "Most actors aren't born stars; their careers must be developed. It's the manager's belief in the young actor that quite often enables her to live up to her potential. Many managers put up their own money to develop actors whom they believe strongly in. They act as mentors, coaches. Managers have a more personalized relationship with their clients. They are more instrumental in career decision-making policy than agents are. They offer legal as well as financial advice to their clients, and introduce them to talent agents, casting directors, publicists—anyone who can be of help in moving the actor's career along. They arrange for auditions for their clients either from the daily breakdowns, through agents, or with specific casting directors whom they work with." Generally, managers work with only five to twenty-five clients. Personal managers are, according to Purcell, "in it for the big haul." They are not looking for the immediate commission. What they're interested in is, "What will be the impact if this artist succeeds?"

### Contracts and Commissions

Generally, managers request that an actor sign with them for three years, with an option at the end of the third year for another two years. The reason for this lengthy time period (longer than the standard agent's contract) is because it can take a long time to develop and create interest in a (sometimes) unknown actor. Sometimes the manager will help the actor along by paying for better training, a better wardrobe, or new headshots.

Because of the abundance of time and energy (and sometimes money) that they invest in their clients, managers charge a slightly higher commission. The average commission is 15 percent. That's not saying that it can't be higher—it can be as much as 25 percent. It really has to do with the specific situation and the particular actor and manager. It should also be mentioned that the percent that a manager receives is in addition to the 10 percent commission that the agent receives (if they worked together).

### Warning

Because managers are not franchised by the actors' unions, there are occasionally unscrupulous and unethical managers who take advantage of innocent talent. As with talent agents, it's always a good idea to ask to see a manager's client list. Also, you should ask around, find out what type of reputation the manager has. Please check out the National Conference of Personal Managers. Their Web site is *www.ncopm.com.*

# Interviews with Personal Managers

**M**ARILYN GLASSER (**MG**), of Basset Talent Management in New York City, spent eight years at Paramount Pictures. She was at ICM in business affairs for seven and a half years, where she worked on contract negotiations. The last year and a half at ICM, she was an agent. She presently handles about fifteen clients.

SID GOLD (**SG**), of Goldstar Talent Management, has been in the business over sixteen years. Prior to that, he worked in the New York school system.

SCOTT E. KREINDLER (**SK**), of Cyd LeVin and Associates, decided to become a personal manager after working with a talent agency for a while and considering being an agent. This company has been in existence for twelve years and handles a limited number of clients.

---

## What does your job entail? What does a personal manager do?

**MG**: A manager's primary function is to provide guidance and counseling to talent. That includes anything and everything, starting with the actor's presentation. I work mainly with new talent. If she's an up-and-comer, that means I help her learn what to do out there in the industry. How to look, how to walk, how to talk. It's teaching her that the minute you walk through the door, your audition begins (and knowing what that means). I took a girl who had been in this town for five years with nobody paying any attention to her. She had a lot of problems. She had personality problems, turned casting directors off. We had to address those problems. What I do is tell actors things they don't always want to hear, but sometimes it's necessary. Telling them things like the fact that their acting is not where it needs to be. If the bulk of the feedback I receive on their auditions indicates that they have talent but need to develop more, I tell them that point-blank. I believe in training anyway, as an ongoing process. I know who the good acting coaches are in this town. I audit their classes if they permit me to. I am a great networker, and I make it my business to find out who's out there teaching. I'm up to date on the best speech coaches, movement classes, improv classes, etc. It really has to do with what the client needs. I'm also available to help the client with wardrobe. Many actors don't know how they should look. So, as you can see, I deal with all aspects of the actor's career.

**SG**: We have an ongoing project of looking for and placing new talent in TV, film, theater, voice-overs, jingles, and print. We introduce actors to agents, casting directors, and producers. We also get them auditions. Our office will do a number of things to promote our talent. We have showcases with our clients in them. We invite casting directors, agents, producers. We do a lot of things in terms of promotion that agents can't or won't do.

**SK**: A personal manager and an agent do very similar things. On a very basic level, the agents get the actors their appointments. The manager helps the actors decide if they're going to go on the appointments. We are also involved with getting appointments for the actors and managing their careers. We help them to determine what's right for their careers, step by step. We have relationships with about twenty-four different agents. Anyone can hang a sign on his door and say he's a personal manager. Everyone here has either been an agent or has an agency background.

## Where do you find your clients? What do you look for?

**MG**: It varies. Sometimes they're sent to me by agents, by other actors. I also find them at showcases, going to the leagues from the big schools, on Broadway, etc. I look for self-confidence. Someone who walks through a door and has an aura about him. Naturally, you look for talent and star quality.

**SG**: We go to a lot of showcases. We also go to theater camps like Stage Door Manor or French Woods. We get a lot of recommendations for talent. Sometimes we advertise in *Backstage*. It really depends on what kind of project we're working on.

When we're looking for kids, we're looking for outgoing, fabulous personalities. With adults, we look for a good look and some experience. With kids, it's easier to get them started as long as they have the personality. With adults, I find it a little harder.

**SK**: Anywhere. Everywhere. Agents will call me with clients whom they feel need a manager. Let's say the actor just got a starring role on Broadway. The agent will call me to see if I might work with his client. There are two different kinds of clients that we will represent. We represent actors who have grown to the point where they need a manager. Perhaps the agent feels that if the actor doesn't get a manager, he (the actor) will move on to a bigger agent. We get the most satisfaction, however, out of developing actors' careers before they even have an agent. When you see star quality that just needs to be developed, it's very exciting.

## What should an actor look for when searching for a manager? What shouldn't he expect from the manager?

**MG**: It's important that actors look for managers who have been in the business for some period of time, who understand the parameters. You want a manager who "gets you." You want a manger who knows what's going on both in this town (New York City) and in Los Angeles, who has his finger on the pulse of the business. Actors should know what contracts are about. You should feel that the manager has the ability to sell you to casting directors, directors, agents, producers. The manager is a third eye for you. When you sign with a manager, you're no longer just with one individual who is in control of your career (the agent). It's really a team effort working for you.

**SG**: First of all, look for someone who's ethical, legitimate, and so on. Preferably, the manager should be in the Conference of Personal Managers. Actors should look for someone they feel they can get along with, someone they can trust, someone who they feel can really do something for them.

All managers do is get actors auditions. You'd be surprised at how many actors seem to feel that it's our job to get them the jobs.

**SK**: A personal connection. Both the manager and the client should feel a passion for each other. Bottom line, the actor must feel a real trust in the manager. She must be willing to believe that this person is trustworthy and will be a strong guiding source for her career. There are actors who believe that once they have a manager, they don't have to do anything for their careers anymore. It'll just all be in the manager's hands. They give over the responsibility to the manager. That's just not the way it is. Actors must realize that it's a team effort. Actors must be out there looking for leads all the time. They can't wait for the agent or manager to do it for them.

**How do you decide which jobs are right for your clients?**

**MG**: I don't decide—they ultimately do. To help them make the right choices, I make the actor aware of where he sits on the totem pole of things. Knowing where you are and in what point in your career will dictate the choices. You're always looking for growth and for movement. If you don't have videotape of yourself, you have to get some. You go from featured roles to supporting leads. From the supporting leads, you have to go to leads.

**SG**: After interviewing clients, we try to find out specifically what talents they have. It really becomes about matching up the job requirements with the skills we feel that each of our clients has.

**SK**: It's always decided on a day-to-day basis. The breakdowns come out, we look at them, discuss them, and see what comes up. You try to be creative. As you get to know an actor, you sort of get a sense of what she wants and what she doesn't want. Again, it's a team effort. You must find out what types of roles and work get the actor passionate. Also, it's about shaping a career. You try not to limit an actor to being just a film actor or just a stage actor. You must go beyond that when casting. I have clients who in the same day will go up for a movie, a play, and a TV show.

**Can you describe the relationship managers have with talent agents? Casting directors?**

**MG**: Particularly in New York more than in Los Angeles, there has been a great resistance to managers. But I feel that's starting to change. The same could be said of casting directors. I've had a number of tremendous relationships with agents over the years, and then I've dealt with agents who wouldn't give me the time of day. They just will not work with managers. The agents who are averse to managers will say something like, "I want to have the relationship with my client." Or, "I don't want you to take the client away from me." My feeling is, if it ain't broke, I'm not going to try to fix it. I generally work with bicoastal agents.

**SG**: We introduce our clients to specific agents. Different agents do different things. We presently work with about twelve different agents. Sometimes agents will call us and ask if we're handling anyone who is about eighteen to about twenty-five, such-and-such a type. We'll recommend someone to them. Basically, the same holds true with casting directors. But with most union projects, the casting director will call the union first. With nonunion work, we get a lot of calls directly from the casting directors.

**SK**: There are very few good managers in New York. Part of the problem is that anyone can be a manager. Agents must be franchised (licensed) in New York. I'm with one of the good management agencies in the city.

Another part of the problem between agents and managers is the insecurity that agents feel—that managers are checking up on them. We don't work that way. We just try to do what we can to get the client in. We do our own submissions. Everyone in this office has relationships with the casting offices. So, instead of calling an agent and asking if he's submitted so-and-so for this project, we'll just submit her on our own. If the casting director okays the client for an audition, then we'll call the agent with the appointment information. As I've said, it's a team effort.

**What do you expect your clients to do to help promote their own careers?**

**MG**: Network like crazy. They must do everything that they possibly can to help themselves. They must talk to other actors, find out who's in the know, find the name of every theater company, and align themselves with the best of the best. They must keep up with already developed relationships, keep up their mailings. Actors must submit themselves for those nonpaying projects because you never know where the great opportunity is going to come from (even student films). At least meet the people doing student films. You never know who they may become—maybe the next Scorsese or the next Coppola.

**SG**: They must be readily available, well trained. We expect the actors to keep up their mailings, reminding people when they've booked work. Part of what they must always do is keep themselves fresh in their contacts' minds. Managers can't be expected to do that for them.

**SK**: First of all, they must be committed to doing good work, constantly staying fresh, taking classes, whatever. They must be prepared and ready for each audition that they get. They must have the confidence for each audition. Part of what we as managers do is instill the confidence in our clients that they need for the auditions.

**If you were to give actors any advice about their careers, what would it be?**

**MG**: Remember, it's a business. Get your ego in check. Understand that you're the new kid on the block. You can do five independent films and everything might seem like you're going to take off and . . . you can be yesterday's news tomorrow. Align yourself with a solid support system, not just flakes.

**SG**: I personally feel that every actor should have a manager. A good manager will get his clients work more than if the client just has one particular agent. If a manager has faith in a client, he won't stop sending her out because she didn't book the last three auditions. Actors should realize that managers are in it for the long haul.

Another thing is, it's not always the best idea to pick out your own headshot. Sometimes it's better to get a professional, subjective eye.

**SK**: I think that most actors have all of their own answers within their own grasp; all they must do is allow it in. Sometimes actors get really anxious and want some secret that will free them up. They must learn that it's within themselves.

# Casting Directors

**T**he casting director's job is to arrange auditions so that actors can meet with directors, producers, and sometimes writers for a particular project. The director and the producer depend on the casting director for their contacts and knowledge of the available talent pool. The casting director often advises the director or producer as to an actor's potential for a particular role.

## What Casting Directors Do

It is the casting director's job to understand the casting needs of whatever project it is that he's working on. If it's a movie or play, he must read the script and then consult with the writer, director, and/or producer as to what types they're seeking for each of the roles. The casting director will contact talent agents to discuss which of their clients might be right for a role. For film and TV projects, the casting director contacts the daily breakdown services, which send out their casting needs to agents every day.

Casting directors work in one of several categories (which sometimes overlap):

- **Advertising agency casting directors** work for a particular advertising agency. They cast actors in TV commercials, radio spots, voice-overs, and sometimes print work.
- **Network casting directors** (daytime and primetime) work for a particular TV network. They oversee all casting for the shows on their network. They generally are concerned with the casting of stars and up-and-coming stars for their network's shows.
- **Independent casting directors** work as freelancers in commercials, movies, and theater. In some cases, they have their own offices.
- **Daytime casting directors** are hired to cast contract roles as well as day players for their particular shows. Their casting assistants cast the under-fives as well as extras.

What follows are the mailing addresses of the New York and Los Angeles daytime serials. They request that you contact them only by mail. DO NOT telephone!

### Daytime Casting Directors

The New York shows are:

*All My Children*
320 West 66th Street, New York, NY 10023
Casting director: Judy Blye-Wilson
Under-fives and extras: Robert Lambert

*As the World Turns*
1268 East 14th Street, Brooklyn, NY 11230
Casting director: Mary Clay Boland
Under-fives and extras: LaMont Craig

*Guiding Light*
222 East 44th Street, New York, NY 10017
Casting director: Rob Decina
Under-fives and extras: Melanie Haseltine

*One Life to Live*
157 Columbus Avenue, 2^nd Floor, New York, NY 10023
Casting Director: Julie Madison
Under-fives and extras: Victoria Visgilio

The Los Angeles shows are:
*The Bold and the Beautiful*, CBS Television City, 7800 Beverly Blvd.,
Suite 3371, Los Angeles, CA 90036
Casting director: Christy Dooley

*Days of Our Lives*
NBC Studios 2 and 4, 3000 West Alameda Avenue, Burbank, CA 91523
Casting director: Fran Bascom
Atmosphere: Linda Poindexter

*General Hospital*
ABC Television Center, 4151 Prospect Avenue, Los Angeles, CA 90027
Casting director: Mark Teschner

*Passions*
NBC Studios, 4024 Radford Avenue, Studio City, CA 91604
Casting Director: Jackie Biskey
Under-fives and extras: Don Philip Smith

*The Young and the Restless*
Bell Dramatic Serial Co/Corday Productions, Sony Pictures Domestic
Television, 7800 Beverly Blvd., Suite 3305, Los Angeles, CA 90036
Casting director: Marnie Saitta

### Interviews with Daytime Casting Directors

MARK TESCHNER (**MT**) has been the casting director for *General Hospital*
since 1989. He also cast the recently cancelled daytime show *Port Charles.*
He has been an independent casting director for fourteen years. *Rolling
Stone* magazine described him as "an actor's casting director." For his work
on *General Hospital,* he has received four Artios Award nominations
for Outstanding Achievement in Soaps Casting. Teschner is on the

Board of Governors for the Academy of Television Arts and Sciences, and is also the vice president of the Casting Society of America.

JIMMY BOHR (**JB**) was the casting director for *Guiding Light.* He is also a professional director. His directing credits include the original production of *Beirut, Romeo and Juliet* at the New Jersey Shakespeare Festival, and productions at the Roundabout Theater, MCC, as well as other regional and Off-Broadway theaters.

VINCE LIEBHART (**VL**) cast contract players for *As the World Turns.* He also cast the Off-Broadway show *Stomp* (three companies). He's worked with David Gordon on his piece *The Mysteries and What's So Funny?,* which was done at Serious Fun and at the Joyce Theater. It won an Obie and a Bessie. He has also worked with Philip Glass.

FRAN BASCOM (**FB**) is currently casting *Days of Our Lives.* Prior to that, she cast *Designing Women, Evening Shade, Hearts of Fire, Women of the House,* and *Lou Grant.*

Note: You'll notice that in some cases, the casting directors' answers to a particular question are the same. Such repetition is a pretty good indication that the advice should be taken to heart.

---

### What do you look at first on an actor's headshot?

**MT**: I want to see what that person is about, not what that person is trying to be. A good headshot should look like an actor at her best, as opposed to how she would like to look. It's something in the eyes, something in the look. It's not about selling, it's about being. The photo should capture something in that actor that makes me want to meet her.

**JB**: Most importantly, it should look like the person. I look for someone who looks very much alive, very relaxed. If it's a picture with a "bitchy" attitude, then one assumes that that's all you can do. I look for something open, honest, natural, with some life to it.

**VL**: It really depends on what I'm looking for. I look for some sort of vitality. But I wouldn't encourage people to do something really goofy. I've seen effective headshots that clearly express the actor's individual personality without being too splashy.

**FB**: Trained actors seem to come across better in their photos than inexperienced ones. Perhaps it's their confidence that's captured. I don't feel actors need three-quarter shots or full-length shots, although I must admit I've seen some very good ones.

### What do you look for on an actor's resume?

**MT**: I'm partial to theater. What plays they've been in, where they've worked, what regional theater, what roles they've played, all of that interests me. The training is also very important. Particularly for young actors who haven't worked much yet, I want to know if they're presently studying and with which teacher.

**JB**: I'm particularly interested in training. I'm also interested in the kind of work someone has done. I like to see the quality of work. Interesting work begets interesting work, and certainly training helps with that. I look at the theaters the actor has performed at or the films or television shows the actor has done. I hate to see plays listed and not know where they were done. *The Importance of Being Earnest* at the Guthrie is a little different from *The Importance of Being Earnest* at the Huntsville Little Theater. Not that I'm making a judgment about that, or saying that there couldn't have been a good production there. But where you've worked, the television shows, the films, the nature of the work—is all determined by the show itself. This includes the theaters, directors, playwrights. If an actor doesn't have much experience, I just focus on the training.

**VL**: I always look for training.

**FB**: Education and training is of significance to me. That's what I glance at first.

**How do you suggest actors make themselves known to you? What do you recommend they don't do?**

**MT**: I strongly believe that you can't make someone see you. Obviously an agent helps, but many actors do get to meet casting directors without them. Actors must constantly create work for themselves. They should always challenge themselves and try to work in a venue where they can be seen. I don't believe in gimmicks. I don't like receiving unsolicited phone calls. Actors should not send photos and resumes week after week. You should send a photo and resume and then follow up a month or so later with a postcard letting me know what you're up to. Maybe a new photo six months after that. I want an actor who's confident in his work as well as with who he is as a person.

**JB**: Gimmicks of any kind I think are foolish. The only real measure of an actor is how he acts, period! It's much more exciting for me when I get to know someone I don't know by seeing them onstage or in a film. I don't want or appreciate gifts from people I don't know solely to get me to notice their resumes.

**VL**: Don't call me! Pictures and resumes initially. Notification of any plays or if you're in any episodic work. Don't drop by!

**FB**: If an actor is in a play, I suggest he send me a flier or phone number and leave the information with my assistant. I go to a great deal of theater. I am inundated with pictures and resumes, and it's impossible to give each one the attention it may deserve. I feel that an actor should not make a nuisance of himself by phoning incessantly.

**What determines whether you'll see an actor in a show or not?**

**MT**: There's not one thing. It's a random selection process. An actor whose work has intrigued me and I want to see more of, a play that I want to see, a theater company . . . all of these things. I will go anywhere to see a play. You always want to make sure the flier is professional-looking. I personally prefer to see a play that has more actors in it rather than fewer. I cast a lot of my day players from people I see in the theater.

**JB**: I like to see good theater, period. If the show is bad, don't expect me to come see it even if you're giving a really good performance. I much prefer to see real theater than to see "scene nights." I'll go anywhere if it's something good. Reputation of the actors, the theater, the playwright, the directors, reviews, word of mouth—all inform me.

**VL**: If I like the play, if I've heard that the showcase is good, if my interest is sparked by the actor, the writing, whatever.

**FB**: My availability. I try to see several actors in a play. A one-man show is not as rewarding for me. I don't go to be entertained. I go to see the actors. Location of a theater is also a factor, since it is virtually impossible at the end of a workday to get to a theater on the other side of town.

### Any specific actor dos and don'ts?

**MT**: I respond well to confidence—not arrogance. I respond to an actor who has a strong sense of who she is—a presence—and, of course, to good work. I don't respond well to actors who emanate a neediness, who telegraph that they need the job. If an actor isn't confident in her work, or at peace with who she is, then she needs to work on that to succeed in this business.

**JB**: I look for artistic choices that actors make. As I said, the only thing that gets my attention is good work. I feel I'm very sympathetic to actors. I understand the difficulties.

**VL**: I really expect an actor to be prepared. I don't expect a scene to be memorized for an audition, but I do want the actor to have given it some real thought. Don't make apologies. I'm open to any questions that actors may have at the audition. Actually, one thing that really bothers me: I always ask, "Do you have any questions?" I don't mind if they don't have any questions and just want to do the scene.

But sometimes, you just feel that they're searching for something to say because you've asked that question. Another pet peeve is when an actor gets my number and calls and asks, "Can you give me your address? I want to send a picture and resume." If every actor did that, I'd never get any work done.

**FB**: My main pet peeve is to have actors arrive for auditions without a picture and resume. This happens frequently and it makes me angry. I don't mind as much when they come without a photo, for whatever reason, but I do mind not having a resume to refer to. The whole interview becomes difficult to conduct.

### When interviewing actors, what do you look for?

**MT**: I look at their energy, their sensibility, their sense of themselves. I want to feel that they're comfortable dealing with me. I rarely do generals because they don't tell me that much about the actors' talents.

**JB**: I do general interviews all the time. I'm not "looking for" anything. I'm essentially very open to whatever it is they want to give me. In an interview, I want to know about your work, how you deal with your career, what work you like, how you approach your work. I want to know what kind of artist you are, and what that means to you. I don't particularly want to know about your personal life. I want to know about your professional life. I think it's important to be able to talk about the work you've been doing, to be able to talk about the work you'd like to do. And I don't just mean about a good job that makes me a lot of money. "My favorite role was this, and this is why. The best artistic experience I ever had was this, because . . ."

**VL**: I rarely have general interviews, but when I do, I look for some sense of personality. The interview is in the actor's court a lot. What I look for is, what can he bring to the show?

**FB**: An outgoing personality is helpful. It makes the interview pleasant to conduct, and one gets to know and remember that particular actor when a role comes up. Actors who contribute nothing to the conversation and give one-word answers will not make a lasting impression. Good grooming and a nice appearance are also vital.

### When auditioning actors, what do you look for?

**MT**: Talent, first. Craft, ability, someone that can take what's on that page and find a way to own it. You must fit the concept, the sensibility of the role. Also, I look for a certain presence, a charisma. Sometimes an actor comes in and even though she is a bit uneven in her craft, there's something compelling about her. She has a strong presence.

**JB**: Talent! Strong, clear choices, command of the language. There are so many actors who, when auditioning for daytime, think they don't have to talk. A lot of actors who audition for daytime think you can mumble. I can't tell you how many actors mumble through an audition. I want to say, "I can't hear you!" Command of the language is imperative no matter what medium of acting youre in. I look for a strong emotional availability at the audition.

**VL**: Because of the nature of daytime, I look for personality. I look for it to be part of what they've brought to the scene. In daytime, actors don't get a lot of input, so actors must have the ability to create something with the scene.

**FB**: I hope actors will have good cold-reading abilities. I also expect them to be able to make adjustments at the audition. If the actor gives a good audition, you always remember him—if not for this role, then certainly for parts in the future. If he doesn't have the right look, he won't get the job, no matter how good his audition is.

### How do you prefer actors maintain contact with your office? How often?

**MT**: Every so often, an actor can send me a note or postcard letting me know what she's up to. Use the postcard as an opportunity to let me know what you've been doing. A generic hello is fine every couple of months.

**JB**: If I don't know you, there's no reason to bombard me daily with pictures or postcards. A postcard tells me nothing about you. If we know each other, then remain in contact when you have something to tell me—when you're in a show or film, or on TV. I tend not to forget people.

**VL**: Only contact me when there's something new or if you're in a show. I discard pictures of people I don't know unless there's some unique skill on their resume that I might need. If there's a picture and resume with a lot of stuff on it, I might keep it because I feel that perhaps this is an actor I should know.

**FB**: Just send a postcard from time to time updating your activities.

**If you had just one tip to give to actors regarding their careers, what would it be?**

**MT**: You can't sit back and wait for your career to happen. As a fellow casting director once said, "Each actor is president of his own company. He has to do something actively every day for the benefit of his company."

The other thing: Love to act. Do it because you love it and not for any other reason. All the rest is illusive. Stardom, financial success are all just byproducts. An actor has only two things—her talent and her dignity.

**JB**: Work as much as you can. I think that those people who spend most of their lives marketing themselves are not real actors. If you're good, you're going to be noticed.

**VL**: One thing that I feel is that schools and conservatories do not prepare actors for this profession. Julliard and Yale should be teaching the business of acting. When actors come to New York, they do have to make a living. Many actors don't even know what an agent or manager does.

**FB**: Get together with your fellow actors and work on scenes, keep on studying, just keep going. Don't give up.

### Interviews with Theater, TV, and Film Casting Directors

SHIRLEY RICH (**SR**) is an independent casting director. The films she has cast include: *Kramer vs. Kramer; Saturday Night Fever; Serpico; Rachel, Rachel; Taps; Three Days of the Condor;* and *Tender Mercies.* Her casting for TV includes: *American Playhouse* ("André's Mother," "Ask Me Again"), *Prince of Central Park,* and *Ryan's Hope* (original cast). For theater, she has cast, among others: *Ballroom, Crimes of the Heart, Sly Fox* (casting director, national; consultant, Broadway), and *God's Favorite.* For Hal Prince, she cast *Fiddler on the Roof* (three companies), *Cabaret* (three companies), and *Zorba,* and she assistant-cast *The King and I* and *South Pacific.*

RISA BRAMON GARCIA (**RG**) is an independent casting director in Los Angeles. She has been directing plays for twenty-seven years and casting movies for seventeen. Some of the films she has cast include: *Desperately Seeking Susan, Fatal Attraction, JFK* (eight films total with Oliver Stone), *Speed,* and *The Joy Luck Club.* She feels that she is primarily a director, and that casting is her "waitressing job."

LORI OPENDEN (**LO**), formerly Senior Vice President of Talent and Casting for NBC, is now a freelance casting director working on *8 Simple Rules* for ABC and as a casting consultant for UPN television.

PETER GOLDEN (**PG**), Senior Vice President of Talent and Casting at CBS in Los Angeles, oversees the casting of series, pilots, movies of the week, and miniseries. He started out with Hughes Moss Casting in New York City. Eighteen years ago, he moved to Los Angeles to work at Universal in the casting department. Next he went to Director of Casting at NBC, then worked as Head of Casting for Grant Tinker's company, GTG, then for Stephen Cannel as Head of Casting, and then in development for John Landis.

MARC HIRSCHFELD (**MH**) is currently Executive Vice President, Casting, for NBC Entertainment. He received an Emmy Award for casting on the HBO miniseries *From the Earth to the Moon.* Previously a partner with Meg Liberman, he cast *Seinfeld, The Larry Sanders Show, Third Rock from the Sun, The Nanny, Mad TV, Party of Five, Grace Under Fire,* and *Married with Children,* among others.

RONNIE YESKEL (**RY**) is an independent casting director. She casts for film, TV, and theater. For TV, she cast three seasons of *L.A. Law* and *Dangerous Minds*. Some of the films she cast were *Pulp Fiction, Reservoir Dogs, Things to Do in Denver When You're Dead, The Long Kiss Goodbye, Hope Floats, Montana, Dr. Bean,* and *The Underneath.*

BERNARD TELSEY (**BT**) at Bernard Telsey Casting works with Will Cantler, David Vaccari, Bethany Berg, Craig Burns, Christine Dall, Tiffany Little Canfield, and Margaret Santa Maria, casting for film, theater, TV, and commercials. Broadway: *Rent, Aida, Hairspray, Long Day's Journey Into Night, Anna in the Tropics,* Baz Luhrman's *La Bohéme,* and many more. Film includes: *Finding Forrester, The Bone Collector, Pieces of April,* and *Camp.* TV includes: the NBC series *Whoopi.* Telsey's company also casts for The Atlantic Theater, Signature Theater, McCarter Theatre, Drama Dept., Hartford Stage Company, and MCC Theater, among others. Telsey is Co-Artistic Director of MCC Theater, which produced *The Glory of Living, The Mercy Seat, Intrigue with Faye, The Grey Zone,* and *The Distance From Here.*

PAT MCCORKLE (**PM**), of McCorkle Casting, casts for theater, film, and TV. McCorkle Casting has been involved with such diverse projects as *A Few Good Men,* productions at the Roundabout Theater, *Ghostwriter* for TV, many of the *Lifestories* for HBO, and the *Remember WENN* series (American Movie Channel), to name just a few.

STUART HOWARD (**SH**), with Stuart Howard Associates, casts for theater, film, TV commercials, and videos. The company's first show was *La Cage Aux Folles.* "Our two favorites," says Howard, "were *Gypsy* on Broadway and *Gypsy* on television."

CHARLES ROSEN (**CR**), a Clio Award winner, is a graduate of Emerson College and has led a thriving and diverse career in the entertainment industry for over twenty-five years. He worked for the Fifi Oscard Agency in 1975, and by 1988 had extensive experience with the advertising agencies Compton and Ogilvy & Mather. Charles became an independent casting director in 1989, and his casting experience has covered every area. He has done television *(Moolah Beach)*, film (Tribeca Film Festival nominee *The Lucky Ones)*, extensive print campaigns (History Channel, Kmart, IBM, McDonald's), commercials and voice-overs (MCI, *The Sims,* Ford), musical theater and plays for Off-Broadway (*The Last Session*) and regional houses (Cherry County Playhouse, Riverside Theatre, Florida Stage), as well as the national tour of *The Presidents,* starring Rich Little. Charles's most recent venture is as one of three partners in the newly formed theatrical production company CRW Productions.

Note: When responses to certain questions are repeated by several casting directors, take notice! It's a good sign that this is something you should pay attention to.

## What do you look at first in an actor's headshot?

**SR**: One thing I must mention: Lately there has been a trend toward this unshaven look for men. I don't like it at all. Basically, I just want it to look like the actors—no *if*s, *what*s, or *but*s.

**RG**: I look for an intensity and a focus. I want to see if the person is photogenic. I look for an intelligence in the eyes. Can the person grab me? I want to see confidence. I look for a lot of things. If I don't see everything, then I usually move on.

**LO**: I just look at it and wait for something to grab me. The eyes first. I look at all the pictures we get here (and there can be hundreds), and throw most of them away.

**PG**: Naturally, I look for something interesting in the face. There's not that much that you can tell from headshots other than if they're attractive and hopefully some sense of how old they are.

**MH**: I try to get a good sense of the personality, of who the actor is. I don't like things that are distracting, like hands in a three-quarter shot, or distracting clothing or background.

**RY**: The soul. Sexuality. You can tell a lot about somebody in a photo. I'm not concerned about the style of the photo—just that it looks like the person. What makes me go absolutely ballistic is when I call somebody in from a photo and she doesn't look anything at all like her picture. I look for interesting, quirky, offbeat faces.

**BT**: I like the three-quarter shots because they show the body. And now they're doing the photos horizontally, which I personally like the most.

**PM**: It depends on what I'm looking for. It depends on what the needs of the role are. In a feature film, the "look" might be more important than certain skills.

**SH**: I look for a natural quality. I just want the person to look like the photo. No surprises when he walks in the door.

**CR**: You know, a lot of people choose shots that are down or at unusual angles, but the actor should be centered in the photo.

**What do you look for on an actor's resume?**

**SR**: I'm an old-fashioned lady about training. I think an actor should be trained in the classics. I believe in a college education. I hope that the actor has some repertory training. Seven seasons of stock isn't the answer for me.

**RG**: I look for theater. I look for work on movies that I would consider to be quirky, interesting, sexy kind of stuff. I look for work in New York and England. If I'm working on a comedy, I'll look to see if they've done *Saturday Night Live* or Second City or if they've worked with the Groundlings, or *Exit 57* in New York. That will get me interested. The comedy stuff will speak to me. I want to see who they've trained with. People who have done theater in New York and Chicago usually grab me. That's my background, and I feel strongly about it.

**LO**: I want to see if they've done classy movies or shows. I want to see if they've worked with directors I know and respect. Like if they've worked for Barry Levinson, who we work with here (*Homicide*), that impresses me. I also look at the training and see who they've studied with. College is very important to me. Yale School of Drama, Carnegie Mellon, and Julliard certainly attract me.

**PG**: I look for a variety of different credits. I'm always looking to see their training. Next, I look to see what work they've done in the business and with whom.

**MH**: Primarily, I start with the television and film credits. I want to see what shows they've done, what directors they've worked with. With theater, I look to see if they've done comedy, if they've worked with Second City or an improv group, that kind of thing.

**RY**: The first thing I go to is theater. Then I go to film to see what they've done and who they've worked with. Next, I look to see where they've studied.

**BT**: I look for some sort of personal connection that I can make. Like some show that I personally saw, or a name that I can identify. Like if I knew a director, say Brian Mertes; if his name was on a resume, I'd have some connection. It's an information tool rather than a credit tool. I always tell actors to put as much as you possibly can on them. You never know who it is we might know. If actors lie on their resumes and I catch them, they begin with a strike against them.

**PM**: The thing about it, really, is there are no tricks to this—and actors want tricks. It's about being the best person for the job. It really has to come from the training and the background on the resume. In an ideal world, everybody would get a chance to rehearse the part and play the part, and then we'd decide whether we'd want to hire them or not. But that ain't gonna happen. So we're trying to get the best person for the role, given the needs of the producer and the director. Actors have to learn that actors act and directors direct. Directors are not acting coaches who are going to tell them how to play the role. Actors have to know what the actor's responsibilities are. And that includes a variety of ways of playing the role and being flexible.

**SH**: Specific credits that might influence the specific audition. After training, I look for major credits.

**CR**: I look at it in much the same way that an agent would. I look at the name, contact number, height, and weight on each picture. If that information isn't there, I have no idea who that person is.

**How do you suggest actors make themselves known to you? What do you recommend they don't do?**

**SR**: For several years, what I've been doing is using the office of whichever producer I'm casting for. I don't have an office per se. I limit what I see to recommendations. If someone I respect says, "You must see this actor," I generally will. For instance, Michael Thomas (the agent) told me about Edward Norton (the actor). He told me I really had to see his work. I went down to the studio where Norton was doing scenes. Then I watched this incredibly gifted young actor do his work. Two other actors, Sean Penn and Robert Downey Jr., also affected me that way. I was delighted to be able to help their careers. Those three are in a class all their own. Getting back to Edward Norton. Since he wasn't in a play at the time, I asked that he show me everything. I knew that he did dialects, classics. And in that one hour, he greatly impressed me.

Over the years I've been all over. I'd go Off-Off-Off-Broadway if I heard an actor was that special. But I do request that actors not invite me to shows with a lot of profanity or nudity. It offends me. Also, actors make the mistake of inviting casting people to shows that they're not great in or have very small roles in. What's the point? You shouldn't be that desperate. Actors must be as selective about the showcase they're in as they are with anything else in their careers. I'm not saying that they shouldn't do a showcase just to keep themselves tuned up. Actors must also learn what they're good at and what their limitations are. Getting back to your question, I don't like when actors send me postcards just to tell me they exist.

**RG**: Postcards are a waste of time. I don't even look at them. If people are doing interesting theater work, especially here in L.A., where it's a rarity, that's important to me because I come from a theater background and I respond to that. A snappy flier to the play will get my attention. Don't do those showcases—the ones that you pay to be in.

I think they're a waste of time. For me, it's really about networking, but in a creative kind of way. Let's say someone is in a play and he really takes his theater work seriously. Then he gets together with other people and someone knows somebody that works for me. Here's an example: Tracy Villar. I've known of her for a long time and thought she always did good work. She did great work in a *Naked Angels* production out here recently. Everybody I know saw it and talked about it. We talked about it and we brought her in and she did a slam-bam audition for us. Other people had seen her over at Paramount for the movie I'm directing. Now her name has come up seriously for the project and her name is on the list. None of us in this room had seen her in the play, but we all heard how great she was.

**LO**: Don't call me. The best thing an actor can do is to keep working. If you don't have the luxury of working in movies or TV, then in theater.

**PG**: Probably the best thing that they can do is let me know when they're doing a theater piece. Not a scene showcase night. If they're in a film or in something on TV, let me know. Do not send a lot of unsolicited headshots or tapes.

**MH**: The best way is to get into a theater production, then send me an invitation with good reviews. I go to theater, comedy clubs, and improv groups. If I get a photo and the look is unique, that could get me interested in the actor. I look at all my mail. What I don't like is actors stopping by. Some actors think that constant phone calls are good—they're not!

**RY**: I recommend they don't call unless I know them. I suggest they send a picture and resume and a letter. If they know somebody who knows me, mention it (and be truthful). We just can't be inundated with a thousand calls. If it's somebody I know and she wants me to see something she's in, then I suggest she call. I can make a plan to see her right there.

**BT**: If it's an actor I don't know, I suggest writing me a really good business letter introducing himself to me. I get a hundred to two hundred resumes a day. Let's assume they're all people introducing themselves to me. Well, if there's nothing on the credits that's going to make the resume stand out, then obviously, a really good letter of introduction describing what the actor is specifically looking for is more effective than a general "hire me." For instance, if someone writes something very specific—like if she says, "I'm new to New York, I graduated from so-and-so, I have no agent representation, and I'm aware that you cast *Food Chain*; if you're ever casting an understudy for Hope Davis, I'd love to be seen for it"—that automatically lets me know that that woman has a clue, as opposed to just a blanket resume in the mail that says "hire me," or, "I want to replace Hope Davis." I mean, the person who asks to be seen for the understudy already shows to me that she knows. Obviously, it doesn't mean she doesn't want to be the replacement, but she knows there are a million working actresses we know already that will probably get that part. Lying or crashing an audition are things I really dislike.

**PM**: I become interested in people by seeing their work. I don't like actors who try tricks to get my attention. Deal with me at a professional level through my office. Postcards and fliers are still the best way to keep in touch, to let me know what you're doing.

**SH**: The difficult thing, of course, is that they have to have work for us to see them. I don't think it's wrong if you're an understudy, for instance, and you're only going on today, to call us. You obviously can't wait to go through the mail. But mailing is always the best. I don't like actors who call for no reason. Many actors have the mistaken notion that when we hear their names, if they call enough, we'll audition them. I think it's the opposite; it's a turnoff. Actors I don't know who send me postcards are wasting their time.

**CR**: Don't phone. Postcards are the best way. Original submissions should be eight-by-tens. Then after that, follow up with postcards.

### What determines whether or not you'll see an actor in a show?

**SR**: As I've mentioned, I won't see a show with nudity or with profanity. I only go if there's a strong recommendation by someone

I totally trust. If someone from my past sends me a flier and I've always loved his work, perhaps I will go. But mainly to Off-Broadway. Very rarely do I see showcases.

**RG**: I don't see that many shows anymore. But people in my office do. It depends on if the show is classy. New work is good. Doing a revival of *Barefoot in the Park* is not going to get much attention.

**LO**: Within my casting department here at NBC, there's me and three other casting directors. We see as much as we can. One of the casting directors goes to the comedy clubs. And the other two cover a lot. I watch a lot of TV. I look to see on the flier if the play has a good director, a writer I like. If the show is too far away, I probably won't be able to go.

**PG**: If it's a show with a relatively large cast, I'm more prone to be interested. Same thing if it's a theater group that I know or admire or if it's a director or writer whose work I like. I'm generally more inclined to see a comedy than a drama.

**MH**: Something that strikes me personally about the show, or word of mouth on it, or good reviews. Other things are, if it's a play I haven't seen by a director I like, if there's another actor in the cast whose work I like, if it's a writer I like. All of those things affect my decision.

**RY**: In New York, I used to go to the theater six times a week. Not out here. If it's a good play and there's good word of mouth on it, I'll go. I'll go to the Mark Taper, good plays, things like that. I'm a single parent, so I can't be out a lot.

**BT**: Timing, how interested I am in that actor, or how interested I am in that show. I go to shows that have a lot of actors I don't know in them. If a show has a lot of young men in it and I'm presently casting a production of *Biloxi Blues*, the timing is right. If a show has a lot of Latinos in it and I'm casting a Latino play, I'll go.

**PM**: They have to do projects that are of interest to a casting director, a play with a lot of actors in it, an interesting writer, a good acting company, a safe locale (where it's produced). We're always looking for new people. But you have to remember that casting directors are human beings. They put in long, stressful days, and that they have to be treated as professionals.

**SH**: I think that mostly, we like to see new plays. There are some companies that have good names. I'm not going to go to an address that I'm frightened of, that's for damn sure. Companies such as MCC, York, Atlantic, WPA. In our office, I send the assistants and interns to the school class nights such as the ones at the American Musical and Dramatic Academy (AMDA) and Circle in the Square.

**CR**: Length of the showcase is very important. If it's going to go on for three and a half hours, and it's hot, and there's no air conditioning, forget it. We won't see *Hamlet*. The opposite is also true. If it's cold and there's no heat in the theater, forget about it. Just keep it short and sweet. We can tell within the first few minutes whether you have talent or not.

**Do you have any specific actor dos and don'ts?**

**SR**: At open calls at Actors Equity, when actors are totally wrong for a part and come to the call "just to meet me," that's wrong. Also, don't talk a lot. Just come in, say hello, do the audition, say thank you, and leave. No excuses, no apologies, please. Don't come to an audition and say, "I have a cold and can't sing well today." If that's the case, cancel the audition. Don't waste our time. Dressing for the part isn't a bad idea (within reason). If that helps the actor to feel better for the part, then I feel that he should. After I've told you everything I know about the character, if you feel the need to ask the director what he has in mind for the part, I think you absolutely should. When actors would ask the late film director Frank Perry what he had in mind for the character, he'd say, "I'll tell you after." He never did, of course. If an actor can be extremely creative with what he sees in the moment, there is a magical audition. When Sean Penn auditioned for the movie *Taps*, he was really not what we had in mind. They were looking for a Philip Barry type. His agent, Mary Harden, begged us to please see him.

And I trusted her taste. Well, Sean made choices at that audition, was incredibly creative, won me over. He thought of all these things to do. I remember he had this soft-drink can and made such interesting choices, such interesting behavior for that character. It blew my mind. I rushed him to Stanley Jaffe and said, "You must see him." Long story short, he got the part and a career took off.

**RG**: Stopping by doesn't work at all. Actors calling me at home isn't a good idea either. I don't like getting accosted in the super-market. I used to get accosted in New York a lot in the lobbies of plays or in bars. It's not as bad out here. Being overly aggressive and stalking are also things I don't like. People can be very desperate here.

**LO**: I don't like being stalked or approached in a restaurant unless you really know me. We make ourselves fairly accessible here in the office, but outside, please, no. The obvious things like "be prepared" and "be on time" are always important for actors to know.

**PG**: To me, it's all about sincerity. I'd rather have an actor be quiet and reserved than overly showy. To the extent that I can gauge, I'd like to see that they're being themselves.

**MH**: The thing that's most infuriating is actors who show up for an audition unprepared. Especially when they had a script available to them and didn't bother or have time to work on it. It wastes every-one's time. Also, actors who show up late, or forgot their pictures and resumes—things like that. Something I like is when an actor keeps the audition simple, doesn't complicate it.

**RY**: I love when actors are prepared. I love when they do their homework. When they're given a script and they go home and take the time to get into the character, create a life. I love to see them come into the audition having made choices. I don't like when an actor doesn't do his homework and sort of wings it. He must take care of his craft, his voice. Do all the things that will make him a better actor. I like people who take chances, who don't care what people think.

**BT**: Be as prepared as you can possibly be for an audition. I watch too many actors pick up the sides five minutes before an audition or not know what the right sides were. If we can be prepared enough to get the appointments out a day or two or sometimes up to a week before an audition, you want the actor to be prepared too. It's such a waste of time when someone says at an audition, "I didn't get a chance to read the play." There's not enough time to see everyone at an audition as it is. Also, don't blow off an audition. If you can't come, cancel it.

**PM**: I hate when actors are unprepared. I hate excuses. I'm not happy when actors don't update their phone numbers, don't update their union contacts. That drives me crazy.

**SH**: I can't bear it when actors put their postcards in Christmas cards. If I don't know you, why are you sending me a Christmas card? My real major, major pet peeve is actors who don't take the profession seriously. Actors who are unprepared, late. When I was at Ogilvy & Mather a long time ago, we did a survey in conjunction with the union. We found out that 41 percent of actors are late for auditions. Forty-one percent! And we're not talking three minutes here. When I first came into this business, whether for a commercial, a play, or a movie, you always came early. You should be there with enough time to get yourself into a good place emotionally. To prepare. I would say seven out of ten actors come in from two seconds before their auditions to fifteen minutes late. Also, I should mention that I very much admire strong choices.

**CR**: Actors should come prepared. They should be ready to do the work. They should come in, prepare, and not socialize. Take the script, make some choices. So when your name is called, you are really ready to go in. In an audition situation, I need to move people. According to the union regulations, I have an hour to get you in and out. Also, I rent studios based on what I'm doing. I don't need people wasting time. Be aware that I'm not there to be your buddy. Most studios that you rent are not well equipped as far as soundproofing. So if you're talking and joking and laughing, it all bleeds through the door and interrupts what I'm doing. Also, don't berate yourself. Don't tell me that this is a terrible picture or complain about how your resume isn't updated yet. Don't whine or tell me that this was just a little role in such-and-such a play.

**When interviewing an actor, what do you look for?**

**SR**: In the old days, I used to interview actors all the time for a film. These days, hardly ever. Just some basic interview questions.

And here are some basic things to remember: Be on time, please. I have a thing about punctuality. Excuses of any kind are not smart at an interview. No apologies. Just try to be open and friendly. Most of all, present yourself as a professional, not as a kid.

**RG**: Presence, self-assurance, confidence, a positive attitude.

**LO**: There's a natural charisma that you find, where you know it's just going to happen for these people. I met Julia Roberts and Meg Ryan early on in their careers. Julia just glowed when she walked in; Meg had a special presence you couldn't miss.

**PG**: Again, I look for sincerity, for commitment to the craft. A big turnoff for me is actors who say, "I'm not interested in stage work. I just want to work TV and film."

There's something very organic about an actor who comes in the room and lets down whatever mask she may be wearing. I know that she feels that there's a lot riding on it. And that's why general interviews are really more valuable to me if I've seen the actor's work.

**MH**: I have general interviews, but I don't find them as valuable as a specific audition. I'm very open at the interview. I respond to the actor just like I'd respond to meeting someone in a personal situation. Is he interesting to me? Does he have anything else going on in his life besides being an actor? I like actors who are also artists and musicians, who have a life. I like to see if they're smart, intelligent, well rounded.

**RY**: Humor. I love somebody who's just down-to-earth, who's funny, and who I can relate to. I like actors who I can just hang out with, talk about anything.

**BT**: Once a week I interview actors. I always look for something that will connect me to the actor. I like to see a person who has a sense of himself. I look for a personality. It's still a people business. It's not just talent or looks.

**PM**: Half the time actors come in, they have no idea who you are. They have no idea what projects you work on. We have to do our homework about the actors, so they should do some about us. No one wanders into IBM and asks, "What do you do here?" You see, it's very easy to fail as an actor, because it's hard to succeed. The options are so limited. If there is a specific project I'm casting that they're interested in, they should bring it to my attention. Usually, I already know what it is.

**SH**: It's a whole other craft, being interviewed. The ability to sell yourself by being honest, straightforward, simple. And charm doesn't hurt. Too many actors don't know who they are. They interview like accountants. They sit there and want you to ask them questions. They don't know how to present themselves. I think the worst kind of interviewee is a passive interviewee.

**CR**: I'm looking for someone who is very much there. I want a firm handshake and I want you to look me in the eyes. And the minute I open the door for you to ask a question, just take off. I'm not sitting there with people who are waiting for me to draw their personality out. I need to ask just one question, like, "I see you did so-and-so. How was it?" Then, *bam!* The actor should just take off. Tell me about your favorite role. What are your dream roles? Be ready to be talkative.

**When auditioning actors, what do you look for?**

**SR**: The most important thing you must remember is that casting directors are looking for a quality—not a performance. Be creative. As I mentioned before, Sean Penn came in for *Taps* and showed us something entirely different, something that wasn't on the page. We can read; we know what the script says. It's the actor who's daring and comes in with something above what's on the page and makes fully committed choices. Of course, I must see an actor who can relate to the character. Just going out on a limb is not enough if you don't know the inside of the character on the page. You must be able to expand what is on the page, enlarge it. I always read with the actors who audition for me. I've never hired a reader in my whole career.

**RG**: I look for someone who is really all about the work, not about all the bullshit. I want to see someone who's focused on the work and has a real sense of himself. It's amazing how people sabotage themselves. They say things like, "I just got this yesterday and didn't have a chance to look at it." Or, "I didn't have a chance to read the script." Or, "What are you guys looking for?" When people start just chatting, it gets kind of stupid.

**LO**: Talent! Knowing how to make a scene work, how to make themselves believable. Adding something to the scene that others didn't. Actors should make strong, definite choices and go with them. And, at the same time, they should be open to directions if they're given an adjustment.

**PG**: I look for actors who are listening to their auditioning partners or to the reader. A big *don't* for me for actors is having the words so memorized that it's all mechanical. They wait a specific amount of time before they respond, etc. It's all too rehearsed, too planned, not spontaneous or in the moment. I like to read with actors because they're paying attention to what I'm saying. And if I take a beat between a certain line reading and they've jumped over my words, it's because they're so rehearsed in it. Nerves, particularly by the time they get to a network, are something that we have to take into consideration. I always look for previous work that the actor has done that I can show to the executives if I feel that his audition didn't come off well. If I've seen that actor in a film project or in TV or theater and he doesn't hit it in the room, I'll do everything I can to help him. With those actors whose work I know and who don't audition well, I try to come to bat for them with the executives by saying things like, "This actor just doesn't audition well. Listen to the voice. Does the height work for you? Does the age work for you?

Physically, is he the right type? You're not going to see it in the audition. I know this actor's work, though." A lot of actors look at the audition as a work in progress. There's an immediacy about television. The time from when an audition takes place to when a role needs to be cast to getting the show on the air is so small. Sometimes wonderful actors need to speed up the process that they'd usually take. At an audition where an actor might just be getting comfortable in the idea of what the role is, he's expected to give a finished performance. But the reality of doing TV is that actors are constantly given new pages just minutes before they're about to shoot the scene. At these auditions, actors are lucky to be given the scenes the day before the audition.

**MH**: I look to see if the actor has a clear understanding of the character. I want to see strong, intelligent choices. Do they understand the context of the scene? Actors don't need to bring in props for the audition. Also, don't work on a lot of blocking; it's unnecessary. Some actors think if they fumble over a few lines, they've blown the audition. The words are the least important part.

**RY**: It depends. Sometimes, actors are in character when they come into an audition. If I can pick that up, if I get that, I'll tell the director, "Let's just go into it, and you can talk after." I like it when an actor tells me that he'd rather talk afterward if he's already in character. Although some directors like to chat first, if I see the actor's in character, I let them know we'll talk after. I always provide actors as readers so that you always have somebody to read off of. At the audition, I'm looking for choices, for colors, for layers. As I said, I love actors who take chances, make choices that are interesting, and go for it. Also, you always look for the actor who didn't make the obvious choice. Humor, even in a scene that may not call for it, can add a lot. Humor can encapsulate a lot and it really endears you to people.

**BT**: You look to see if they're prepared, if they have a sense of the project they're auditioning for. During the audition, you're looking for the actor who can perform this role, has all the emotional colors necessary to do this part. The actor who takes that audition scene and can make it as colorful as the whole two-hour play or movie is a real find.

**PM**: I want him to be good. I look for the actor who knows what he's doing, is professional. You want to feel that the actor knows what the material is about. I really hate when an actor comes in, is introduced to the director, and seems befuddled. It's a profession, a business. A lot of young actors just think it's art.

**SH**: Strong choices. It takes a while to see if someone is a yes, but the no is instantaneous. I look for someone who comes into the room and heats it up. And usually that happens more often with women. Men are, by and large, more closed.

**CR**: Creativity and choices. Be the life of the party. Make us believe you know what you're doing. Even if you don't, make us believe you do. You come into the audition with as much confidence as you can, and make us believe that that script was written for you.

### How do you prefer actors maintain contact with your office? How often?

**SR**: Since I don't have an office, there is nowhere to send mail to. There are those people whose work I know very well that let me know what's going on in their careers. If they are in something good, they let me know by mailing me fliers to my apartment. But I don't like mail from people I don't know.

**RG**: If they have an agent or manager, it should be through them.

**LO**: I like the postcards telling me what they're doing. The best way is though their representatives—their agents or managers.

**PG**: If they have a good agent, the agent will make sure that they're in our minds. If they're not represented, a postcard once in a while. On this subject of not being represented, most of the actors I see are represented by agents. Because I'm not online casting, I'm responsible for overall casting of everything on our network. When I worked for Stephen Cannell casting *Wiseguys*, or when I was in New York casting *The Cosby Show*, I would see many actors who weren't represented. I'd say about 50 percent of the actors I saw for *Cosby* weren't represented.

**MH**: I like when actors send me postcards telling me they're in an episode of such-and-such, or this movie, or this play. Even if I can't catch the show, I get a sense of awareness that they're working. Hearing from an actor once every month or two is fine. But just dropping me a line saying, "Hey remember me?" is really not too productive. If you have something to tell me about, that's the best time—even from an actor I don't know. If I get a card from an actor I don't know letting me know, "I'm appearing on *Will and Grace*, or in this play," it piques my curiosity about him or her. Maybe I should get to know him.

**RY**: Notes. I move around a lot, go from job to job. We don't have a permanent office yet. Once I get my permanent office, I know I'll be inundated. But I do like personal notes, people filling me in on what they're doing. But actors should only contact me when they have something monumental to tell me. If it's somebody I know, however, I like to know what's going on with him.

**BT**: I think maintaining contact with the office is very important. It may have been someone I worked with a while back and just forgot. I look at every piece of mail. Postcards are very good ways. Every eight to twelve weeks is a good amount of time, since you're always starting a new project about every two months. Unless it's commercials, which we do every week. I encourage actors to keep in touch. That postcard that comes in at the right moment, just when you're looking for that type—*bam*! Get her in tomorrow for the Maxwell House commercial! Or it might be, Get her in tomorrow for *The Three Sisters* at Hartford! It's okay to say, "Just keeping in touch. Anything you're presently casting that I might be right for?"

**PM**: Postcards. Or when they're doing something. If you're on a soap, let me know. I may not have to see the soap, but at least I know you're working.

**SH**: I don't mind the postcards. I don't mind the notes. I think they all work.

**CR**: Postcards, once a month.

**If you had just one tip to give an actor regarding his career, what would it be?**

**SR**: Study. Training. I can't think of anything else that's important. One piece of advice for singers for musicals—be sure that the song that you sing is within your range, without the break in the voice. Never sing something that you haven't studied and studied.

**RG**: Act every day. In class, in workshops, in the theater, making short films for friends. Anything you can do—just keep acting.

**LO**: Be prepared before you start the auditioning process. You can make a lot of bad connections. The way to determine when you're ready is in your acting classes, and just a feeling that I'm ready, it's time. Don't enter the business too soon—it can be very damaging.

**PG**: Act because you can't not act. If you can do something else, then do it. An actor I know once said that the reason he loved auditioning is because it was another opportunity to perform, and he loved to perform. He was lucky just to have an opportunity to audition. Getting the roles were the best thing, icing on the cake. My advice is, take any opportunity you can get to perform. If it means working on a student film. If it means working in a small theater group somewhere. These days, there are no limits as to where a casting director will go to find talent. In terms of supply and demand, the demand is so high. In television, there are six networks, basically, not to mention dozens of cable channels, all looking to schedule original programming, and all looking for actors. Also, always remember acting is a craft that is a combination of instinct and training.

**MH**: Take charge of your career yourself. Don't completely hand it over to an agent or manager and wait by the phone. The whole idea of an actor signing with a manager just to have additional doors open—I don't think it's too smart. A lot of actors sign with managers and don't even know who the manager's other clients are. Ask yourself, What can this manager do for me that my agent couldn't do? It's an unawareness of what their representation is doing for them.

**RY**: Study. Study, study, study, study. And with good people. Always just work with good people. Do theater as much as you can in between. And don't give up. If it's what you want more than anything else in the world—and it has to be what you want more than anything else in the world—don't give up!

**BT**: I have two tips. One is, you must understand it's a business. Treat any communication and contact in that way. Treat it the same as if you were going for a job at IBM. The second thing is, keep yourself constantly involved in a creative atmosphere. That doesn't mean you have to go to the extreme of starting your own theater company, but do start your own Monday-night reading series. Constantly do something creative. Don't spend all your time on self-promotion and losing your art. Do something creative at least once a week. Also, actors should always remember that casting directors are really on their side. We want them to give a great audition.

**PM**: Train and keep training. Keep those juices flowing. Because it's always changing and there's so much that you have to have a background on. Actors should keep working, whether it's showcases or classes.

**SH**: Don't stop studying. I think it's important to work. Geraldine Page never stopped. After she got through with Lee Strasberg, she went to Uta Hagen (or maybe it was the other way around).

**CR**: Try to be two people in your career. Be the actor, the creative person, and also be the businessperson. You have to do the things that are appropriate to get the auditions. Get onto a network to meet people within the industry. Be the businessperson who can sell herself. If you can't be a businessperson, then hire a manager or work your butt off to get an agent.

# Publicists

**A** publicist is involved with many aspects of an actor's career, from molding an image to consulting on career decisions. Publicists arrange media interviews (television, print, radio) and fashion layouts (if applicable), supervise photo sessions, create press materials, and give general advice—all of which help promote an actor's career. Campaigns vary depending on what the actor is doing. Publicists make up press kits that will include the actor's photo, bio, resume, copies of any previous press they've had, etc. The bottom line is that they attempt to make a person famous for whatever it is he or she does.

### Do You Know Who I Am?

When the actor has a substantial role in a movie or play, or has written a book that he or she wants publicized, the publicist will send out press releases to newspapers, magazines, television, and radio. Sometimes, however, the actor gets into legal or criminal trouble. At these times, the publicist tries to keep the client out of the newspapers, or at least give the criminal news a better "spin."

### Interviews with Publicists

MERLE FRIMARK (**MF**) heads her own public relations company in New York City. The personalities she has worked with include Chita Rivera, Sir Ian McKellen, Sir Derek Jacobi, Angela Lansbury, Glenda Jackson, Peter O'Toole, Jessica Lange, André DeShields, Mark Hamill, Jessica Tandy, and Hume Cronyn.

CLAIRE O'CONNOR (**CO**), of the Claire O'Connor Agency, has been a publicist for eighteen years. She has planned parties and garnered headlines for such clients as Mickey Rourke, Johnny Depp, Montel Williams, Governor Jerry Brown, and President Bill Clinton.

---

**At what point in his or her career should an actor contact a publicist?**

**MF**: An actor should contact a publicist when he has won a leading or featured role in a film, a Broadway show, or an Off-Broadway show, is on a television series, or finds himself with a unique cameo role that he feels will showcase his talent. It is certainly more difficult to publicize a chorus member or an actor with a very small role. When deciding to hire a publicist, an actor should not make this decision alone. He should consult with a manager or agent, and interview a minimum of four publicists.

**CO**: I think it's good to start early in a career, but the actor should have something going on. A young actor, not in a show, just starting out, doesn't have much to promote.

**What should an actor expect from a publicist? What shouldn't he expect?**

**MF**: Again, much of this depends on what the actor is doing in which area of entertainment. It is important to always remember that there are no guarantees! Any publicist who says he will guarantee you certain coverage is not being honest, and the actor will probably be disappointed. If an actor can separate her performing persona from her business persona, she will be able to be more objective when planning her future.

**CO**: Actors can expect that publicists will get them press and get their names out there (within reason). If an actor is in an Off-Broadway show, let's say, but with a meaningful subject matter or a trendy or timely subject, he can get better press. He shouldn't expect the cover of *Time* magazine unless he's mega-big. But what he should and shouldn't expect really varies with the actor. One thing that shouldn't be expected, however, is any guarantee. It's all relative to what the actor is doing and what the writer is writing about this month or this year. If the actor has a good product, he can expect plenty of coverage.

## What determines the length of a relationship between a publicist and an actor?

**MF**: This varies greatly. If an actor is in a Broadway show, he may want to retain a publicist for the run of the contract. Many film actors and performers hire a publicist on an annual basis. Many publicists will only take a client for six months or more. Anything less than that is not realistic. A publicist needs enough time to test the waters, make contacts, and distribute press materials. National monthly magazines work three months in advance, and it does take time to generate media interest in any major city.

**CO**: It depends. If you're Bruce Willis, you always have a publicist, because you always have something going on. If you're constantly working or are a big star, you should always have a publicist. On the other hand, if you're going to do a show next month and you want people to know about you (and it), you may want to hire a publicist for that month, or hire her for a longer period to do follow-up. For example, you can be doing a show and hire a publicist, and she brings, say, fifty press people to see you. Ten of them may say, "In April, I'm going to be doing a story on young actors." It would be smart to make sure you've kept the publicist, so she can get you in on that story. If you can afford it, it sometimes helps to have a publicist to do events like throw a birthday party for you and invite celebrities. Keeping your name out there even if you're not acting is also important.

**What are the financial considerations? How much should an actor be prepared to spend?**

**MF**: It varies. Different agencies will charge varying fees. However, as in buying good clothing, we all know that we get what we pay for. If a publicist charges an extremely low fee compared to others interviewed, chances are, the actor should not expect high-end results. There are some high-profile stars who retain publicists to keep them out of the press. Regardless, the actor should keep within his or her own budget when hiring a publicist.

**CO**: From about $1,000 to $10,000 a month. It's difficult to say exactly what the actor gets per dollar. It has more to do with how much time and energy he expects from the publicist. Naturally, if the publicist is hired on a full-time basis, she will be making every effort to accomplish whatever it is that the client needs, publicity-wise. Quite often, there are slow periods in actors' careers when there really isn't that much to promote. It's certainly a lot easier to get them in the columns when they've a hot movie or show about to open.

**Is there any advice you have for actors before they contact a publicist?**

**MF**: Actors should be realistic and have an idea of what they hope to achieve from their relationships with a publicist. Oftentimes, there is a relationship that can last for many, many years. They should be aware of their own limitations (e.g., preparing to do many interviews) and be prepared to open themselves up to the press.

**CO**: Actors should be prepared to carry through with it. They should have available time to do the interviews, photo shoots, etc. They have to really want it. You have to allow the publicist to do her job. Mainly, you must be available and willing to follow the advice you get. One problem I see all the time is the actor who doesn't want to do the small TV show interviews. He doesn't realize that quite often, until he's done those shows, it's hard to get him onto the bigger interviews. I have to get a tape of that small show and get it to the bigger ones to show that he's a good interview.

## When selecting a publicist, what should actors look for?

**MF**: It is important that actors feel comfortable with and trust the publicist. This is a relationship based on trust and honesty. Actors should feel free to ask to see the publicist's client list.

**CO**: I think they should choose someone who has the time for them. A lot of big agencies who have a Bruce Willis or a Robert Redford just won't have the time for you. The lesser known actor cannot afford to not get what he wants for his money. Ask around for recommendations. Ask other actors, agents, and managers which publicist they've heard good things about. Then you should interview the prospective publicist. Don't just hire him on the phone after a short talk.

# *Voice-overs*

**A**ccording to David Zema, voice-over specialist, a voice-over is "any voice heard over visuals where you do not see the person talking. For example, the voice or announcer you hear introducing a television network news program, or the voice you hear on a television commercial telling you about a sale at the local department store, are both voice-overs. Narrations of films or multimedia presentations can also be considered voice-overs. Today, radio commercials are also called voice-overs.

"Voice-over performers must have the ability to read copy in a natural way so as to make it sound as if it is being spoken spontaneously, in a believable, sincere, and trusting manner. The reader must sound as if he is personally involved, understands the message, and is communicating it to a specific listener for a specific reason or reasons. Effective voice-overs for commercials, recorded novels, and radio dramas require the ability to create moods and express the appropriate emotions needed to convey the author's message."

### Are Voice-overs for You?

Actors who have been told that they have interesting or unusual voices, or that their voice has an unusual pitch or accent, should look into this very lucrative field. The job of the voice-over actor is, quite simply, to sell a product. Because your face is never seen, this work has a built-in anonymity to it, perfect for those actors who are uncomfortable in front of the camera. Not everyone, however, is right for voice-over work. So, before rushing out and making a voice-over demo, I suggest that you check with agents and casting directors you know to see if they feel that you have potential in this field. Also, check out some of the voice-over schools and coaches, and ask their opinions. This is a very competitive field. If you honestly feel your voice is special and/or that you're willing to work very hard to develop the necessary skills to be successful, then I say, go for it!

### Nine Tips for Voice-over Success *by David Zema*

1. On a daily basis, you should listen to professional voices, noting their performance styles and qualities. Record these voices and try to emulate each performance style.
2. Read aloud daily. Books, magazines, newspapers, and even ketchup bottles can be helpful.
3. Work on a good tape recorder with a separate microphone.
4. Find your own strengths, including the copy styles and products your voice is most suited for.
5. Project your entire personality into your voice.
6. Work on your resonance and diction daily.
7. After developing your strengths, work on opening your vocal and performance style range so that you will be more versatile.
8. Work with a supportive, positive coach on a regular basis.
9. Wait until you have mastered your skills and feel confident about what you have to do before making a demo. Do not send a homemade demo to the top talent agencies.

### Your Voice-over Demo

The voice-over demo shouldn't be more than a couple of minutes long. It's imperative that you have your best work up front. If the agents don't hear what they want immediately, there is a tendency to turn it off. Do at least a few spots in your natural voice. Variety is the key here. Your voice must be very expressive. You must be able to show emotional, dramatic, and comedic changes. If you can do character work, make sure that each character is as brief as possible. That is, establish the character and then get on to the next one. Whichever type of copy you use—original or professional—make sure that it's appropriate for your type of voice.

You should always have your demo done in a professional studio. It can be a bit pricey, about $700 for the whole thing (including session time in a recording studio), but there are always good deals to be found. Just make sure the level of work is professional.

One thing you need to realize is that your first demo tape is not your *only* demo tape. It's something that's going to change. If the demo tape is working for you, you really don't have to make another one. As you start booking jobs, you'll be using sample clips from your work. Select very wisely when you do this. Make sure the sample features you and shows you off well.

You shouldn't put different types of work on one reel. It's basically a field of specialization. In the beginning, try not to be all things to all people. Find what you're best at and put it on the demo. Next, find out who needs what you're best at, and then send it to them. There is much more information on demo tapes in the interviews in the next chapter.

### How to Get Voice-over Work

Use the various trade sources like the *Ross Report*, David Zema's *Voice-over Marketing Guide* and *Production Screen Magazine* (Chicago), and *The Standard Directory of Advertising Agencies*. Each area has its own book of listings. There's also a national directory called *The Motion Picture, TV, and Theater Directory* (Tarrytown, New York).

Before sending out your demo, it's sometimes best to call first, find out who the casting director is, and ask if you may send it. Naturally, agents are very important contacts; don't forget producers, ad agencies, and recording studios either. Think of your tapes as ads. Once you've mailed them out, you probably won't get them back, although some of the big agencies will return them. You should follow up and call the places you've sent your tapes to. You may realize that sending one demo tape and making one phone call may not be enough. You have to follow up with a postcard or a note, then a second phone call, then a third phone call. If you're an actor who works on camera, you might want to also have your photo on your demo box. Also, you can make rounds (go in person to agents, casting directors, and studios) to drop off your demo. Studios, by the way, are also in a position to recommend you for work. Many producers work out of their homes and might be offended if you show up there, so I don't recommend that you do that.

### Dispelling Voice-over Myths and Misconceptions

So many actors are afraid to look into the lucrative field of voice-overs because of fears of inadequacy or misinformation. Voice-over specialist David Zema says, "I'd like to squelch some of those fears." Below, he provides answers to common questions.

- *There is a belief that only strong voices are needed for voice-overs. Is that true?* There is a great demand in voice-overs for comedic and character work. They are always looking for "quirky" and "interesting" voices. There's no doubt, however, that having a good, strong voice is a plus.
- *Another belief is that no one trains for this type of work—either you're born with a great voice or you're not.* Some people who have been told that they have good or interesting voices have the misconception that all they need to do is open their mouths and sound pretty. Even mellifluous or quirky voices need training. It's not so much the voice or what you're saying; it's how you say it. Voice-overs are like singing: You have to know how to use your voice.
- *Are voice-overs basically just "reading copy"?* The key is to make it sound natural. It's not always easy to be conversational and enthusiastic under pressure. It takes supreme confidence.
- *You rarely hear women announcers. Is the voice-over field sexist?* There are a lot of women in the voice-over field, especially in cartoons. Women's voices are well suited to cartoons because of their flexibility. I'm not saying that there has never been sexism in the field of voice-overs, but women have made

great strides in the past twenty years. Female voices are used more and more.

- *Is training really necessary for voice-over work?* Not knowing how to use your voice correctly can be damaging in the long run. Placing your voice in the throat to make it sound deeper is the sign of an amateur and can irritate the throat. It's better to train and develop a natural range and resonance that produces a pleasing voice without tension.

# Interviews with Voice-over Specialists

**D**AVID ZEMA (**DZ**) is a voice-over performer, producer, and coach with twenty years of experience. His voice can be heard in many commercials, cartoons, and industrials.

GLENN HOLTZER (**GH**) teaches voice-overs at Weist-Barron (a theater, television, and film school with branches in New York City and Los Angeles) and also does private coaching. He trained as an actor for twenty years and has been teaching for seventeen (including fifteen years at Weist-Barron).

## What kind of training should an actor have before making a voice-over tape?

**DZ**: A good voice-over coach can help you where the studio engineer can't. A coach should have a good idea of exactly where you are marketable. I personally think the best way for someone to learn voice-overs is private training. A voice-over class can tell you what the basics are: how to handle the copy, how to handle the auditions, how to take direction. A class teaches warm-up exercises and teaches the actor the different styles of copy. Private coaching, however, is far more beneficial. You get a lot of microphone time, learn how to take direction, learn different ways to handle the same material, and learn different techniques. A coach can also help you learn where your blocks are and teach you how to sound more natural.

**GH**: Before starting any voice-over training, I think it's important to have an acting background. I think acting classes are very important for the voice-over artist. True, there are some actors who are natural voice-over people who can learn as they go along, but that's very rare. Actors with theater training seem to learn voice-over work faster.

I teach actors to apply their acting work to the script. Don't be fake. You must talk to one person, put your personality into the work, connect to the copy, know the text (you can't just read), and know who you're talking to. The story must have a beginning, middle, and end. Part of what I teach is that you must make it personable, as personal and as conversational as possible, through whatever format they're asking for. Whether it's "up-energy" or "sexy" or "first-person" or "character," your job is to make it believable. The main thing is it must come from you. It's not just announcing and reading well. That's why 95 percent of voice-over performers are actors.

**What is the price range for coaches and classes?**

**DZ**: Classes can start as low as $250 for six classes and can go up to $900 or $1,000 for the ones that include a demo tape. Coaches are as low as $40 or $50 per hour and can go as high as $60 or $95 for the top people.

**GH**: Anywhere from $50 to $125 an hour for coaches. Weist-Barron charges $350 for ten classes. Generally, that seems to be about the going rate.

## What things should an actor know before making a demo tape?

**DZ**: Get good, clear guidance. Find someone you trust, who can help you. You'll need someone who knows about the market and can help the actor see where he fits in. Sometimes you can't really see that yourself. If you know a casting director or talent agent who knows your work, he or she might be of some value to you. Basically, I think that actors make a lot of mistakes with their demo tapes. They rush out and get a voice-over demo without really designing it. Just as people should put in time with their headshots, they should also be selective about their demo tapes. This is a marketing tool, an advertisement for *you*.

Actors often go to the first studio they find and do a demo tape without ever asking if the studio does actor voice-over demo tapes. It could be a music studio they've gone to. It wouldn't be appropriate. The studio wouldn't know how to mix the music appropriately, or even know the correct copy. Avoid studios that use a copy file. These pieces of copy have been around forever. That same copy is on many demos.

**GH**: Almost every agent that has come to Weist-Barron to talk to my voice-over class has said that 95 percent of all voice-over tapes they receive end up in the garbage can. What they're saying is that most voice-over tapes are not good. If the tape is good, you had better be able to back it up with a good audition. You must be able to nail a read on the first take, because you only get two or three shots at it.

## What are the initial expenses in making a demo tape, and how much time do you need to allow to set it up?

**DZ**: Everyone does it differently. There are these places where you can take a six-week class and come out with a demo tape costing you about $1,000. But I definitely say, do not do that unless you've already done the private coaching and the other stuff we've talked about. Some studios have package deals. Generally, it can range from about $300 to about $500. It usually takes about two to three hours in the studio. Some places produce the whole thing right there and give it to you then. Other places may make you come back on another day. Generally, the copies can be as low as $1 a tape, up to $3 a tape.

**GH**: Actors must be very well prepared before they go into the studio. Make sure that those reads are prepared and down and ready to go. Demos can be made for as little as $250 or $300 and can go as high as $1,000. For over seventeen years, I've been doing voice-over demos over at Full House Productions. They do all the demos for Bloom, Cunningham, ICM, Paradigm—all the big agencies. I charge my fee ($65 an hour) and their charge for talent is $75 an hour. It usually takes about three or four hours.

### What would you say the criteria should be for selecting a studio?

**DZ**: It should be a studio that does voice-overs and records them for radio and TV. Don't go to a music studio or to someone who only does industrials. The engineer should be familiar with voice-overs. He should have recorded auditions as well (so he knows what the casting directors are looking for). He should be comfortable mixing voice-overs, music, sound effects, whatever. You also need someone at the studio who can direct you, so that you know what is currently marketable.

**GH**: It should be a full-service studio, not just a studio that does demo tapes. Use a studio that specifically has had experience doing voice-over demos. Also, find a studio that is used to doing ad agency work. Aside from Full House Productions, the only other studio in New York that I recommend is Star Tracks.

### What are agents looking for on a demo tape?

**DZ**: The number one thing is, Is it marketable? Marketable in advertising means, What is the current trend? Advertising has trends. Like, the "Generation X sound" is very big now. Some others in the past have been announcers, spokespersons, those kinds of things. In the eighties, a big one was the Molson Golden couple—the flirtatious husband-wife, boyfriend-girlfriend, kind of Stiller and Meara thing. Another one is the guy who was doing the Alamo voice-overs. He had kind of a poetic style that was popular for a while.

**GH**: Anything and everything. Whatever the agent needs for his roster. Whatever style he feels is selling. It really depends on the actor as to what he puts on his demo. If the actor is good with character voices, I suggest that he highlight that on tape. Range is not necessarily important, but conciseness is.

### What do voice-over casting directors look for?

**DZ**: Much of their concern is whether you can handle the job, are at a certain professional level. They certainly can tell from a demo tape whether you're ready.

**GH**: Pretty much what I said before for agents. Also, casting directors usually refer to agents.

### How long should the demo tape be?

**DZ**: A commercial demo is around two minutes long. A promo is really short, under two minutes. A character demo will be a little longer because you have several characters. An industrial tape will be a little longer, closer to three minutes. They want to make sure that you can sustain the reading. Also, the medical tape will be closer to three minutes.

**GH**: A minute and a half to two minutes.

### How many different types of promos are there?

**DZ**: Medical-technical, industrial (financial, training tapes, infomercials), CD-ROMs, films (under narration), commercial demo, commercial character, and cartoon character demo (mostly used in L.A.). Also, if you do foreign languages, have a tape for that. The new tape these days is the promo tape (announcers—big on the cable channels, as well as on talk shows).

**GH**: Now there are commercial demos, promo demos, character demos, and narration demos.

### What kind of money can you make in this field?

**DZ**: The top people, these promo announcers, make six figures. But there are no residuals, and they have to work every day. But generally, a good voice-over person can make $50,000 to $60,000, up to $100,000 and more.

**GH**: Side money (part-time) in voice-overs can go from $10,000 to $15,000 a year (and more). Full-time, you can make up to a few million a year. The sky's the limit. There only are a few overnight successes. It usually takes a few years to start making real money. There are probably five or six hundred people in New York trying to get voice-over work today. So, sometimes it can take a while to make some real money in the field.

### Voice-over Schools

**Voice-over Edge Studio**
251 West 30th Street, Suite 9-FM, New York, NY 10001
(888) 321-EDGE
*www.edgestudio.com*

**Ruth Franklin**
(212) 496–9696
(no Web site)

**Marla Kirban**
630 Ninth Avenue, #110, New York, NY 10036
(212) 397–7969
*www.marlakirbanvoiceover.com*

**Steve Harris**
New York City
(212) 517–8616
SteveHarrisNY@aol.com

**David Zema**
135 West 26th Street, 2nd Floor, New York, NY 10001
(212) 675–4978
*www.davidzema.com*

# Working on Daytime Serials

**W**ork on daytime serials can be very rewarding for an actor, both financially and professionally. Some of Hollywood's biggest stars started out working on the "soaps." Alec Baldwin, Meg Ryan, Kevin Bacon, Kevin Kline, and Kathleen Turner are just a handful of actors who benefited from the exposure that they received on a daytime serial. Because an entire one-hour show is shot in one day, the challenge for actors (as well as everyone else involved) can be quite intense. Yet there are actors who not only work on a soap during the day, but also find the time (and energy) to work in the theater at night. For one, Larry Bryggman, an actor who appears on the daytime serial *As The World Turns*, constantly appears on Broadway.

There are different categories of acting jobs available for actors in daytime. They are:

### Extras

These are actors who do background work on the show. They do not have any lines. You'll mainly see extras in restaurant scenes, airport scenes, hospital scenes, funeral scenes, and busy office scenes. Every week, many actors are hired for extra work on the shows. When there are wedding scenes or courtroom scenes, the number can increase quite a bit. Extras should be seen and not heard, and they should be careful not to cross (unless directed by the stage manager) between the camera and the main actors in the scene.

### Under-fives

These actors literally have five lines or fewer. They fill non-contract roles such as delivery men, waitresses, shopkeepers, police officers, and bank tellers. Some under-fives can recur (sometimes for years). What's difficult about under-five work is that you have to create a character with very little dialogue. The secret to these roles is to not try to make too much out of them; don't try to milk the moment in any way.

### Day Players

These one-day roles have over five lines and can be recurring. If they do recur, and if they become important enough in the story line of the show, the actor may be asked to sign a contract.

### Contract Roles

As the name implies, these roles are played by the stars of the show and are continuous. For how long? It depends on the contract that the actor has been offered. Generally speaking, most new character contract roles tend to go to younger actors. These can be wonderful opportunities for actors new to the business. The new character roles created for older characters are usually given to actors who have substantial acting experience.

Actors who are seriously interested in work on daytime serials should try doing some extra work first. By doing extra work, actors can get a sense of how the day is structured on soaps, and what the studio is like to work in. Actors who don't aspire to speaking parts on the soaps are quite content to do extra work. Some of these actors are hired with regularity by the casting directors for scenes that recur in hospitals, offices, and police stations.

# Producing Your
# Own Play

**O**n occasion, a group of actors, or a single actor, finds a play that truly moves them, and they decide to mount a full production. To be done well, a project like this demands a great deal of time and energy. The cast and crew must believe that the play can be fully realized with integrity and artistic truth. To just do a production to "show your wares" quite often results in half-baked production values that look shoddy. The last thing you want is for your production to be labeled a vanity production. You and your company must be of the same mind and same vision.

### What Are Scene Showcases?

Rather than producing a full-length play, occasionally actors will get together and produce a "scene showcase night" targeted at talent agents and casting directors. This is a team effort where all involved have agreed to put their time, energy, and money into a project created expressly to show off their talents.

The selected scenes may be related by a theme or totally arbitrary, depending on the needs and talents of the group. Generally, one of the actors in the group is selected to be the main producer; otherwise, chaos may ensue.

Usually, the group votes on all artistic and economic decisions concerning the event. A director and stage manager are hired or volunteer from within or outside the group.

### Things to Keep in Mind for a Scene Showcase
The group must decide on the following:

- A budget and how much they are willing to chip in for this event. Scene showcases can cost from several hundred dollars per person to over a thousand.
- A theater.
- How many nights the show will be performed.
- What kind of refreshments will be provided for the invited audience. This can be as simple as wine and cheese, or be much more extravagant.
- What jobs each member of the group will do. These volunteered chores include everything from mailings and phone blitzes of agents and casting directors to painting scenery, buying and setting up the refreshments, and managing the stage and house.
- Casting.
- Selection of the order of the scenes.
- What kind of follow-up to agents and casting directors is needed after the event is over.

### Producing

To produce a play in a showcase situation can be very complex and demanding. If it's a new play, there can be many months of rewrites and development before a production should be mounted. If your group is optioning a play (paying royalties), there should be a few readings to see if the play works well for the actors. In both instances, you might want to think about a fund-raising benefit to help with the costs of producing.

Again, I think it's important to mention that this kind of venture should stem primarily from a love of the play, not as a means of promoting yourselves as actors. That being said, here are some things to think about before taking on such a large task.

### Skills Needed to Produce

- **To produce a play, you must have good organizational skills**. You will be arranging everything from casting to hiring a director to raising the money for the production to finding a theater. You must be a person who can deal with minutiae. The producer is at the top of the totem pole. It's your vision that can either make or break the production.

- **You'll need excellent business skills**. It'll be your responsibility to raise the money for your production and to handle all the expenses. Part of having good business skills is being able to negotiate with people, keeping accurate financial records, etc. The average Actors Equity showcase costs between $10,000 and $20,000. It's advisable never to use your own money, unless you can afford to take on such an expense. In some cases, the members of the cast either all chip in or do some type of fund-raising event to get the money for the production.

- **You must have promotional skills**. Unless you have the ability to get people to come see your show, it'll be a somewhat wasted effort. Getting newspaper critics, for instance, can be very difficult. You'll want to get agents and casting directors to come see your work—also not an easy task. Even getting a good audience night after night can be quite a chore. You must start your mailing and phone campaigns way in advance of opening night. The whole thing is a matter of persistence, diplomacy, and tact.

### Exactly What Does the Producer Do?

- Oversees the budget for the show
- Hires or finds a director
- Finds the theater
- Arranges for the casting of the show
- Hires or finds a scenic designer
- Hires or finds a lighting designer
- Hires or finds a stage manager
- Is responsible for all legal obligations

- Hires a publicist if financially possible
- Finds the best insurance for the production
- Hires a ticket agency if it fits into the budget
- Is responsible for having tickets and programs printed up
- Finds rehearsal space for the actors
- Has to deal with any problems with the cast, the director, the scenic designer, and the landlord

### The Reading

Don't produce a show unless you've had at least one reading (preferably a few) of the play. In the case of a new play, what looks good on paper doesn't always make for a good evening of theater. Some plays read well but don't play well, and vice versa. Even if the play you've chosen is well known and has been produced many times, the reading is a great opportunity for you and your fellow actors to experience the roles you'll be playing and to see how an audience responds to the play. Since there will be an invited audience, you'll also be able to get some sense of the production's potential. Use a tape recorder to tape the reading. It's not advisable to invite casting directors and agents to these preliminary readings. The whole purpose of the reading is to try out the play, not to audition for casting directors. Since you'll only have a few rehearsals before the reading at best, you shouldn't expect too much from the reading. If the reading(s) goes well and the response has been positive, then perhaps you might consider going to the next step on the ladder: a fully realized production.

### Preproduction

There are certain times of the year when it is not advisable to open a showcase. The Christmas holiday season (mid-December) through the first week in January is a difficult time to get people in to see your show, as is most of August. If you're planning a summer production in the city (when theater rentals are less expensive), you'll find that your audiences will be thinner, especially on weekends, since many people go away. And you'd better be certain that the theater you've chosen has a reliable air-conditioning unit, or you'll see many people in the audience flee at the first intermission—or sooner!

It's very important that there is constant communication during the pre-production period between the members of the company (as to how things are moving along). Try to keep everyone posted on significant production details as they are arranged. Things like the production dates and the theater must be announced as they are decided, so that everyone is kept abreast.

### Looking at Theaters

One way to begin finding that right theater for your production is by asking around and gauging the theater's reputation. Generally, certain theaters have a buzz on them, either good or bad. If they've been unkind or unfair to actors in past productions, it'll get around. You should also make it your business to start going to showcases around the city to see the different theaters.

#### Criteria for a Good Theater

- Check out the location of the theater. Is it near public transportation? In a pleasant neighborhood?
- What condition is the theater in?
- How are the acoustics? What is the size of the stage?
- Is it well ventilated? Too cold? Too warm?
- Is the house staff polite? Organized?
- Are there clearly marked fire exits?
- Is there an area to store furniture? Props?
- What is the backstage area like? Is it safe? Sanitary?

#### Before Signing the Contract for the Theater

- Remember, no Equity showcase can be performed in a theater that has more than ninety-nine seats.
- Never sign a contract for the theater until you've had at least one meeting with the theater manager to iron out all the details.

- Most theater rental prices are negotiable (if not for money, then for services).
- Be clear on all of the terms of the rental agreement. There should be no gray areas. It is always to your advantage to have a lawyer look at the contract.
- Some pertinent questions you should ask:
  - Is all the equipment in the theater included in the rental, or do I have to bring in anything of my own for a production?
  - Will the actors be given rehearsal time in the space during the day?
  - Does the theater handle phone reservations and have a ticket booth?
  - How far in advance of the performance time can the company use the space?
  - Are deposits refundable?

### Allotment of Money for a Showcase

You will need to budget all expenses for your production in advance. Here are some of the major costs that producers must keep in mind when producing an Equity showcase:

- The rental of the space (the theater). Theaters on Theater Row in New York City can cost up to $3000 per week. Theaters Off-Off-Broadway and L.A. waiver theaters can run $100 to $400 per night. The more out of the way the theater is, the less it will probably cost.
- Rehearsal space. Sometimes rehearsal space included with your theater rental. Generally, rehearsal space starts at $12 per hour and can be as high as $25 per hour and more.
- Insurance for your production. Mandatory by Equity and in most theaters. The amount varies depending on your specific situation and the theater.
- Fliers and mailing expenses. This is your main means of advertising. Fliers should be as elaborate as you can afford. It is, after all, the first impression your potential audience

members get about your production. This can cost your company as little as a few hundred dollars up to thousands of dollars, depending on your budget.

- Costume costs. Sometimes your cast can bring their own costumes. When you do period plays, costume rentals can soar.
- The set for your production. Many companies build their own sets. Once you hire professionals to build and paint your scenery, you're running into a big expense, especially if there are multiple sets.
- Prop costs. Quite often, your cast can bring their own props.
- A ticket agent. It's not always necessary.

### A Union or Nonunion Show?

Somewhere early in the planning of your production, you will have to make a very important decision: union or nonunion. If you yourself are a member of Actors Equity and wish to star in this play, there really isn't much choice. Equity actors may only perform in Equity-approved showcases! Actors who aren't members of Actors Equity, however, may perform in Equity showcases. If you are nonunion and decide to produce a nonunion showcase, you're pretty much on your own. Even if you choose to go nonunion with your show, you still must deal with state health laws, personal/work ethics, public safety, and many other producer headaches. The main advantage you have in a nonunion show is that you don't have the union breathing down your neck with any rules or regulations on how your show must be produced. Also, there is a lot less paperwork.

If, however, you opt for a union show, you have to contact the business representative in charge of Equity showcase productions at Actors Equity. In New York City, the address is 165 West 46th Street, New York, NY 10036. The telephone number is (212) 869–8530. You must apply for your Equity showcase application fourteen days before you begin casting or start rehearsals, whichever comes first.

### The Equity Showcase Code

Actors Equity defines an Equity showcase as "a not-for-profit production in which AEA members elect to participate for the purpose of presenting plays and/or scenes in limited performances for the benefit of participating members."

- The show can only be performed in New York City. (The waiver theaters in Los Angeles have similar rules. Check with Equity for theaters outside of New York City.)
- It must receive the express consent of Actors Equity.
- The show can be produced only by individuals, groups of individuals, and/or not-for-profit institutional theaters that have not been prohibited from doing so by contract or prior agreement. Any producer on the Equity list of defaulting producers shall be not be accorded the privileges of the Showcase Code.
- You can only have up to twelve performances within four weeks (but can get four additional performances if needed).
- Complimentary tickets must be made available to industry people.
- Equity must receive the following information from you prior to your initial casting:
  - The dates of all rehearsals and performances.
  - The cast list (available roles).
  - Either your address or the address of someone you designate where Equity actors can send their photos and resumes for consideration for roles in your production.
- Also keep the following in mind:
  - You must reimburse the cast and crew for transportation costs for all rehearsals and performances that they attend.
  - All Equity members must be comped in (free) to see your show if there are available seats at that performance.
  - Actors in your production are entitled to have their photos displayed in the lobby and a copy of their bios printed in the play's program.

# The One-Person Show

**P**erhaps one of the greatest showcases an actor can have is the one-person play. It is just you alone on the stage in front of the audience. But if your only reason for doing a one-person play is to be seen, please let me advise you here and now—don't. What I've discovered in the interviews that follow is that the only reasons for putting yourself through this extremely difficult and time-consuming process should be the love of the play, the character, and/or the character's beliefs and ideals. If your motivation is purely self-promotional, simply to be seen, more likely than not, you will fail. And a failed performance will be judged as nothing more than a vanity production. The scrutiny you are subjected to in a one-person play is much harsher than it would be if you were part of the cast of a regular play. Forewarned is forewarned.

If, however, you have found or written a one-person play that excites you, then certainly, you should go for it.

Finding producers for your one-person play may be difficult, so you may have to produce it yourself, which is not usually a good idea.

If the play has previously been produced, you may have to pay royalties for each performance. If it's a new work, there may be a period of development and rewrites, with the playwright attending rehearsals. If you've written the play yourself, you'll need a third eye to help you shape the piece, as well as perform in it.

The director you choose to work with on this play must be someone whose opinion you trust implicitly. Because of the nature of a one-person play, you should be prepared for an intimate, intense collaboration with your director. The director's vision must be similar to yours.

And finally, you must be prepared to work for a long time on the play—perhaps years. One way to gauge your progress is to have readings and performances of the piece before an invited guest audience.

As you can see, it's a tremendous amount of work, requiring a total commitment. But if you're determined and your dedication to the play is total, and you have the talent to pull it off, acting in a one-person play can be the greatest theatrical experience of your life.

### Interviews with Actors in One-Person Plays

ROB BECKER (**RB**) began doing stand-up comedy in 1981. In 1989, he appeared on *Late Night with David Letterman*. In 1988, he began working on his one-man show, *Defending the Caveman*. It has had sold-out runs in San Francisco, Dallas, Philadelphia, Washington, D.C., Chicago, and New York City. It was was the longest running one-person play on Broadway.

PAUL ZALOOM (**PZ**) won an Obie for his performance-art piece, *The House of Horrors*. The piece originated at the Dance Theater Workshop and was later performed at the American Repertory Theater in Cambridge. His solo shows were also performed at Theater for the New City, the Performing Garage, the Manhattan Punchline, and the Vineyard Theater. His nine solo shows received eight European tours and numerous national tours. He performed on the CBS show *Beakman's World*, an educational science show for kids (although 55 percent of the audience was adults).

COLIN MARTIN'S (**CM**) show *Virgins and Other Myths* was called "riveting," "emotionally charged," and "remarkably candid" by the *New York Times*. He performed the show at Primary Stages in New York City, and then it moved Off-Broadway for a very successful run. Prior to New York City, the piece was performed in several theaters in Los Angeles, from 1994 to 95. Most recently, he appeared as Prior in *Angels in America* at ACT in San Francisco. Other credits include Charles Ludlam's *Camille* at the Highway Theater in L.A. and guest-starring roles on *ER* and in the films *Crimes and Misdemeanors, Three of Hearts,* and *Majorettes.* He is a member of Artists Confronting AIDS.

---

**First, a little information about your piece. What's it about? Its genesis?**

**RB**: Basically, it's about the gender gap. It's about men and women, their differences, the gap in communication between them. I use my wife and my marriage as an example.

**PZ**: *The House of Horrors* piece consisted of three sections: "The House of Horrors," "Safety Begins Here," and "Yikes!" *The House of Horrors* is a piece about indoor pollution. I was really interested in the idea that the average American home has about four thousand chemicals in it. After we build our houses, we make them airtight to conserve energy, and so we live in this chemical stew. Most of these chemicals are known to be carcinogenic. The piece is a puppet show using dummy or doll puppets about eighteen inches tall. It's about how the house, the carpeting, the couch, and the wallboard all collectively kill the family. It's a slapstick, wild comedy.

**CM**: It's about sexuality, power, and innocence at different points in a person's life—how sexuality evolves and changes. I use the theme of virginity, which is a universal concept or condition as a starting-off point to explore sexuality. I tell my own story, my experiences, my personal journey to explore these themes.

**How did you get it started? How long before your first production? Were you pleased with that production? What did you learn?**

**RB**: I started writing *Defending the Caveman* in 1987. I was doing stand-up comedy and I started including pieces of it in my stand-up routine. In 1991, I put it up at the Improv in San Francisco. It took three years from the time I started writing it until the first public production. I was pleased with the response. It ran for four months. One thing I realized is that it's far different to have something on paper than it is to do it on stage. What looks good on paper sometimes feels a little stiff or uncomfortable on stage. I really had to kind of tailor it to myself. I'd talk to people after the show, get feedback. I had some pieces in there that were really funny and got huge laughs, but then I realized from the feedback that it made the wrong point. In a one-person show like this where there's a theme, a story, a beginning, middle, and end, where you're trying to make points along the way, you have to give up stuff if it makes the wrong point.

**PZ**: I had played at Dance Theater Workshop with my previous program. Dance Theater Workshop is a very good, very visible venue for alternative performance and dance. I asked David White, the producer, if he'd produce my new show, and he said yes. Generally, my shows had a two-year cycle. I did a new show about every two years. A show would be created while I was touring with another show. Money was raised through grants and earned income to finance the new show.

   As far as being pleased with the show? Yeah, it went the way I wanted it to go. And no, I didn't get the response I wanted. I wanted a hit, a long-running Off-Broadway show. And that was not the response I got. My idea was to do the Off-Off thing and get a producer with some money to move it. The joke is that I'm like a television star now and people think that that's the apex of my career, my goal. But to be an independent artist, to create things out of your head, that is on your own agenda, and that makes you nuts—to do that is far more fulfilling. Doing the solo shows was much more rewarding than doing TV.

**CM**: I was in Los Angeles, working with a group called Artists Confronting AIDS. The work was going great but I was broke, thinking I might have to leave L.A., go back home to Madison, Wisconsin, and get a nine-to-five job. I just wasn't interested in becoming a generally successful actor on TV. But, I thought, before I leave L.A., the one thing I have to do is write something. I hadn't written anything since I was a teenager. Simultaneously, I had read a book called

*A Rock and a Hard Place* by Anthony Godby Johnson, a teenager who was infected with AIDS by a friend of the family who had sexually abused him. I was very moved by it. I'm basically a very private person, reticent. But it just seemed like this was the right time. That was the genesis.

**What obstacles have you encountered in performing in your own show? In producing your own show (if you did)? How did you eventually overcome them (if you did)?**

**RB**: It's extremely difficult to get anybody to put on your show when you're new. Finding theater space is difficult. That's why I started in a comedy club. I did produce this show at one point. The problem I had in producing was that the Improv wasn't putting much into advertising, so I had to put some in. Luckily, this show has always succeeded on word of mouth. Because of the show's reputation (from San Francisco), the Improv asked me to do it even though it wasn't finished. The first few weeks were rough. I was rewriting all day long, putting it on stage at night, and then going home to do more rewrites. I didn't have a third act. I'd do the first and second act, and then at the end I'd come out and tell the audience, "Here's what I'm working on." And basically I'd tell them my ideas for that third act. It was weird, but it worked. Even when it was that rough, people were out telling their friends about the show.

**PZ**: My work was not readily adaptable to the Off-Broadway audience. It tended to be more political and somewhat didactic. I was hoping to be relentlessly entertaining, but maybe I was just too low-rent, too eccentric, too out there for Off-Broadway. I was paid by the venue—a fee. There were also the grants. At Dance Theater Workshop, they provide services to independent artists, unlike any other venue in America. They give you a kit that tells you how to produce yourself in New York and gives you guidance on how to build a career.

**CM**: I mentioned to a friend of mine in mid-December of 1993 that I wanted to do this, and she said, "Great, let's produce it!" Realizing she was serious about producing, I wrote the piece in about two weeks.

I set up two workshop dates, January 9 and 16, 1994, at Noho Studios in North Hollywood. I had been producing a theater series there for Artists Confronting AIDS. Ten days before I opened, I got a director, Bruce Blair. The whole thing was a big adrenaline rush. See, I hadn't written any of it down; it was all in my head. A lot of people came to see it and were very encouraging. We got a booking from that production at Highways Theater (Tim Miller's space). And then we held a work-in-progress show at the Zephyr Theater in March. I was afraid that my story would only be of interest to me. I learned that there was interest in my story; other people found it compelling. I realized I had to do work on the dramatic structure and the theatrical integrity of the piece. I didn't want to do just vignettes. I wanted to create a journey, a play with a beginning, middle, and end. I realized I had to be patient, that I had a lot of work ahead of me.

The main obstacle I found was that some theaters felt that any play that deals with gay sexuality is a "gay play." And if one gay play is done a year, that's the quota. People want to pigeonhole plays.

At the beginning, I produced the play myself. Bruce Blair and I were very grassroots. We did a lot of the fund-raising as well as co-producing it with Geo Hartley in Hollywood. I walked the streets and put up fliers, whatever. Everyone should do that. That's what it takes.

### How did you go about finding the creative team for your show?

**RB**: I directed it myself. I had an acting coach come in for the first couple of weeks to give me some notes. So, in a sense, I was my own creative team.

**PZ**: Dance Theater Workshop provides a lighting designer. I hired a consultant, Gordon Edelstein, during the rehearsal period. He had worked with me at the Berkshire Theater Festival. We worked together to polish the piece. It was the first time I had somebody from the outside help out. I went on to have other people to direct later pieces.

**CM**: Originally, my friend Mindy Kanaskie produced it. She brought in Bruce (the director), and my collaboration with him has been invaluable.

**What have you learned from this experience? What achievement regarding this project are you most proud of?**

**RB**: Theaters are sometimes very strange when it comes to business. There seems to be some noble thing about losing money. You can go into these theaters and say, "I have this huge hit, this one-person show." And you get all this resistance because you're not Mamet or someone. The main thing I've learned is you just have to believe in yourself and what you're doing.

**PZ**: My interest has always been to get people to laugh about things that are essentially going to kill them. Lord Buckley (a Beat comedian of the fifties) and Peter Schuman of the Bread and Puppet Theater were my two biggest inspirations. Buckley said, and I'm paraphrasing, "It is the duty of the humor of any given nation in time of crisis to attack that crisis in such a way as to get the audience to laugh so they don't die before they get killed."

**CM**: As an actor, it's the toughest role I've ever done. It's very hard to get up there, be honest, and just connect with yourself. I've learned that when I honor who I am rather than try to change or alter who I am, my life and work take on an amazing energy, and the results are incredible. It's very empowering. If you don't shout out into the world, you can't get a response back, since you don't give the world anything to respond to. The payoff is the letters and phone calls I get from people. When audience members stay after the show and tell me how they've identified, how they've connected, it's very rewarding.

**What advice do you have for other actors considering this type of project?**

**RB**: You have to really believe in your piece. If you really do, other people will, too. You have to be willing to put your own money into it in the beginning. Keep mailing lists. I have a mailing list of fifty thousand. I let my audience know what's going on, if I've been extended, where I'm going next, things like that. That's how I got such a big advance sale here in New York. It was the biggest advance the Helen Hayes Theatre has ever had. I'm a big believer in setting goals. Broadway was a goal I set for myself. [Becker did break the record.]

**PZ**: It's really great being an artist and doing your own art and not having to rely on someone else to write for you. I came from a community of performance artists, where relentless self-promotion was not looked on kindly. I don't advise creating a performance piece to launch yourself into Hollywood. It must be compelling, something you can have yourself. But for an artist to be successful, you must find ways to promote yourself. I was relentless about promoting myself. My approach was to take a lot of photographs. I hired a photographer, did a twelve- to fourteen-hour photo session where four hundred to six hundred pictures were taken. And then I had about twenty-five original and about six bulk prints made up. So there were hundreds of prints offered as exclusives to major papers, and the bulk ones were sent out. Dollar for dollar, it was the best investment possible. The whole thing was a couple of grand, but I got hundreds of thousands of dollars' worth of free publicity.

**CM**: This piece is not about trying to get affirmation or validation of my experiences. It's not about therapy or portraying myself as a victim. I wanted to create a piece of theater that had integrity as a piece of theater. If other actors want to draw from what I'm saying about myself, they're welcome to. But basically, I don't like to give advice.

# Independent
# Films

**T**here are a great many opportunities for actors working in independent films. Aside from acting in them, many actors are now also producing, directing, and/or writing their own movies. For the same amount it would cost to produce an Off-Broadway show, you can now make your own independent film. Many actors have started taking filmmaking and screenwriting classes in hopes of eventually producing, and starring in, their own films.

Chazz Palminteri wrote and performed his one-man show, *A Bronx Tale*, with the specific intention of having it made into a film with him starring in it. Robert De Niro saw Palminteri's show and, indeed, did produce the movie version with him in it. Many actors are taking Palminteri's lead and are writing their own one-person shows, hoping for the same results.

One thing I've discovered in researching this topic is that there are a great many ways to go about making an independent film. Each filmmaker I met with seemed to have gone about it her own way. I felt that to truly give this topic (filmmaking) a fair discussion would take much more than just one chapter in a book such as this. What I think might be more helpful is to refer you to some excellent books on the subject. Also, please check out the actor-filmmaker interviews at the end of this chapter.

### Helpful Books

If you feel that you have the potential to be a screenwriter, I'd like to recommend the following books: *Four Screenplays* (Dell) by Syd Field, *Writing Great Screenplays for Film and TV* (Arco) by Dona Cooper, and *Writing Scripts Hollywood Will Love* (Allworth) by Katherine Atwell Herbert.

For actors with an interest in directing and/or producing films, I suggest the following books: *Making Movies* (Dell) by John Russo, *All You Need to Know about the Movie and TV Business* (Fireside) by Gail Resnick and Scott Trost, *Feature Filmmaking at Used-Car Prices* (Penguin) by Rick Schmidt, and *Shoot Me: Independent Filmmaking from Creative Concept to Rousing Release* (Allworth) by Rocco Simonelli and Roy Frumkes.

### Why Experienced Stage Actors Are a Plus for Independents

I had an enlightening discussion with Robert Hawks, a professional independent film consultant. His company, Independent Consulting for Independents, assists film directors and writers by critiquing their scripts and then looking at the rough cuts to assess what potential they may have in the marketplace. Hawks also helps filmmakers select which festivals the film might be right for and helps select potential distributors to be targeted for a particular film. He has been on the advisory committee at the Sundance Film Festival (as well as many other festivals) and is also a film curator and programmer.

He explained how significant a good role in a well-received independent film could be in bringing an actor's talents to the public's eye. He pointed out that "actors can find meatier and far more substantial roles in the independents," and went on to say that, "Having a strong theater background can be very helpful when working on independent films." Because of the economics involved, these films have to be shot quickly. Often there will only be a couple of takes. The actor must be well prepared. Good theater training is vital. "Some independents have the luxury of a rehearsal period prior to the film's shooting. An actor who's well trained in theater can utilize the rehearsal period to deepen his work on the character and focus his performance. Stage actors know how to rehearse, how to concentrate, how to repeat the same thing over and over without getting stale. They are more disciplined in their craft. Naturally, they are a real plus on an independent film set."

## Ways to Find Work in the Independents

Agents receive daily breakdowns on many of the independent films that are casting. The trade papers constantly list auditions for them. On occasion, some independent films receive readings at different theaters on off nights (Mondays or Tuesdays). Check the trade papers to see when these readings are scheduled.

## Interviews with Actor-Filmmakers

PATRICK INZETTA'S (**PI**) film *Grace Has Mace* was a short (half-hour) black-and-white film. He co-produced, co-wrote, and co-directed this film with Julie Berg. The film has been entered in several national and international film festivals.

MICHAEL NEELEY'S (**MN**) *Badges* is a forty-five-minute color TV pilot.

**How did you get the idea to make your own independent film?**

**PI**: Julie [his partner] had made several short films, and I had acted in several short films. We use to talk about ideas for films, and then one day, Julie said, "Why don't we make one?" So we sat down and started work on the script. This was my first screenplay. It took us a good year to get the script finished.

**MN**: A couple of years ago, a friend of mine and I were driving into the city and were discussing the differences between us. He was Italian, born in Italy, raised in New York, and I was from the Midwest. We started imagining what it would be like if we were teamed up as cops. Then, about eight months ago, I was approached by a director I knew who said he wanted to put together some video shorts for his director's reel. At around that same time, an attorney friend of mine, who had worked on putting together a cable access program that had fallen through, mentioned that he was looking for a project to replace it. So everything kind of fell into place. My friend and I decided that we'd write up the script. The director would get his short for his reel, and my lawyer friend would get a replacement for the project that he'd done all this groundwork on.

### What did you need to know before beginning?

**PI**: We started breaking down how we visualized it, using storyboards. We storyboarded all of our camera shots. Also, we scouted locations in New York. Julie and I were going to co-direct, and I was also going to act in it. Our actors were actors I knew from around. The salaries were deferred, since there really wasn't any money budgeted to pay actors. With things like sound, however, we had to put money up front to pay a sound technician. Sound is important and not something you can skimp on. The film wasn't made as a commercial venture; it was made to show people what we could do, our potential.

**MN**: I was the actor, writer, and producer on the project—a lot of hats. We started having meetings to develop and write a script. We formed a limited liability company. The script took about a month to finish. Next we did a staged reading. We cast actors, rented a theater space, invited an audience, and even had questionnaires for the audience to fill out about the reading. After the reading, we had a question-and-answer period; then, we made some adjustments in the script and set up a time to do the shooting.

### How did you begin? Where do you start?

**PI**: We owned our own cameras, which saved us the rental fees for cameras. We shot on 8 mm. Everything was planned in advance. What we were doing was guerrilla filmmaking. For instance, we didn't have permits or things like that. Julie had worked in an editing facility and later on, we bartered time for editing. You must understand, everything was on a shoestring. We did make up a budget. The price of the film was expensive, as was developing. We edited the film by transferring it to video (and then doing the editing on a computer).

Sound is a big expense. Props, costume, food—these are all things that we budgeted. The film cost $7,000. It took us three years from start to finish (including editing, postproduction, etc.) The reason it took so long was because of everyone's schedule. We met maybe once or twice a month. It was a very loose shooting schedule: weekends, mornings, late at night, whenever we could. The actual shoot took place over one year—probably around forty shooting days.

**MN**: First, of course, there's the budget. You have to figure out what things will cost. You go through each department on the film and see what your needs will be. We wanted to shoot our film on 35 mm, but changed that to a high-grade beta that transfers easily to film. The other major expenses on our film were craft services (meals), editing, and sound. We did the film as a nonunion shoot. We sent full breakdowns to every agent and manager in town. We got a great response to the breakdowns. The casting call took place in three stages: the general audition, the callbacks, and then a screen test. I strongly advise you to screen-test for a movie if you can. We put together the crew at the same time. We got a line producer who scouted locations, got our insurance, permits, etc. Just so you know, the insurance policy is usually $1 million for these shoots and costs about $5,000 (depending on what and how you're shooting). We got our permits through an NYU [New York University] affiliation. If you want to get a permit to shoot, it's not that difficult. You just have to show them proof of insurance and tell them where you want to shoot (your shooting schedule). The shoot took two weeks (six days a week).

### Any advice on the day-to-day shooting?

**PI**: I learned that it's very difficult to direct a film that you're acting in, especially the first time out. It's definitely something I don't recommend to other actors if they don't have to do it.

We did about three takes for each shot. We had to be sure we had it because we were shooting in black-and-white and had different film exposures.

For us, the most expensive thing in the budget was the sound. You must invest in good quality of sound. Another big expense was the transferring of the film.

**MN**: The first day we did stunts. This wasn't the smartest thing to do. I ended up falling and cutting my hand. Also, have everything as prepared as you can. Have it all mapped out. Use storyboards.

### What was acting in your own film like?

**PI**: Wearing the two hats (director and actor) was tough. You know what your character is thinking and feeling, but then there's this other voice coming in and saying, I wonder how this shot looks? I felt that my performance was divided a bit. I found it hard to watch myself on the screen when we screened the film.

**MN**: Acting in my own film was difficult. You have to give up the other hats you're wearing and just be the actor. It's difficult because your mind is on a thousand other things.

### You've finished shooting the film. What next?

**PI**: We sent the film out to be developed as we went along. Next, you transfer it to video. Then it goes into the computer, and that's where you start the editing. Julie was the main editor. You develop a rough cut and see if you like that. Then another rough cut, then another. Next you put your sound in, and a musical score. We promoted it and started showing it around. We had a showing at the Knitting Factory here in New York.

**MN**: After the shoot, our director did the editing of the film. We saved a lot of money on editing because he had access to editing equipment. He made up a rough cut, and then we all worked with him editing the next cut. Next we did some looping and voice-over work. He put some nice titles on it, and then packaging, and then we were through.

**How do you find out about and enter your film in the film festivals?**

**PI**: There's a book of all the festivals and you pick which ones are right for your film. The film is showing right now in the Chicago festival. The fees for the festivals are $25 to $50 (Sundance is $50). You send a press kit with your video and hope for the best. We went to the New York Underground festival, and one in New Jersey. The festivals are really a source of promotion for your film. You don't have to be at the festival where your film is showing. About 70 percent of people whose films are showing aren't at the actual festival. It helps to be there and network with people.

For me, as an actor, making a film was a good way to promote my acting career. First, I postcarded people, letting them know that I made a film and that it's in a festival. Next, I offered to send copies to casting directors. I've actually gotten work from several casting directors who saw my movie. Also, I can give copies of the film to anyone who wants to see my acting work.

**MN**: We won't be entering the pilot into any festivals, but we're going to make a feature (based on the pilot), and that we will enter in the festivals. We will be sending this pilot around, and hopefully someone will be interested.

**Any advice that you might have for actors thinking about making their own movies?**

**PI**: I suggest that you go with professional actors on your film. Hiring friends can create all kinds of problems (even if they are also actors). As a producer, I learned to be diplomatic with the actors and crew if a problem came up. That's something you don't have to deal with when you're just the actor in a movie. I did a two-hundred-piece mailing to casting directors and agents after the movie, inviting them to the New York festival. It ended up getting me some auditions and jobs.

**MN**: Always allow double the amount of time you thought you needed for a shoot. If you think it'll take an hour, give yourself two hours. There's always something that goes awry.

If you're thinking of making a TV pilot, as we did, and it doesn't get picked up, there's nowhere else for the pilot to go. Whereas if you make a feature film (which can potentially be the first episode of a future series), you can have two successes (feature film and TV pilot). When you make a feature film, there are still ways to make your money back.

Rather than producing an Off-Broadway play, you can invest that same money into making a short film, probably with better results. A film is something permanent that you can have. A play will end and that's it.

### Some Insights on Filmmaking from Jimmy Georgiades and Eric Lane

*Jimmy Georgiades (director/producer) and Eric Lane (producer/screen-writer) recently co-produced the film* First Breath. *They had the following to say about the experience*:

First Breath tells a very unconventional love story, one that takes place in a manicured suburban neighborhood. As filmmakers, we felt our challenge was to follow the truth and simplicity of the characters and story. The issue of infant abandonment has reached epidemic proportions in the United States. We tried to address this issue through narrative and characters in a way that hadn't been done before, and explore ideas such as the power of denial, paternal instinct, unconventional love, self-discovery, and truth in friendship. The idea was not to present a simple solution to a problem, but hopefully, to raise questions and issues surrounding it.

There's a saying that in television, the producer is God. In feature filmmaking, the director is God. And we'd like to add that in the world of independent filmmaking, God is the director, producer, cast, and craft services.

Instead of sitting around, waiting for the phone to ring or hoping someone would say yes to us, we decided we needed to create our own work and say yes to ourselves. All those people making the decisions got started the same way. We quickly learned that what you don't have in money, you make up for with your time, energy, and commitment.

If you wait to know everything you need to know before making a film, you'll never make it. We put in countless hours preparing for *First Breath*. We were lucky enough to surround ourselves with wonderful people. What we wound up with far exceeded anything we could have imagined on our own. It's not about losing your vision, but about creating an atmosphere where people feel safe enough to bring their best to the collaboration.

Basically, film production breaks down into four areas of activity:

1. Preproduction
2. Production
3. Postproduction
4. Distribution and festivals

Each area is incredibly important in creating the final film that someone will see. Regardless of whether your film runs three minutes or three hours, you have to go through every step of production.

### Preproduction

If you have the knowledge that your film absolutely needs to be made and that you'll do whatever it takes to get it done, the film will happen. What can seem like an insurmountable obstacle just becomes something to be taken care of.

We found preproduction to be most stressful part of the process, as there were so many uncertainties. Money, schedules, timing, locations, cast, and crew all needed to be coordinated on a shoestring budget. We now understand why film credits runs so long at the end of a movie.

### Production

With most features, it's "Hurry up and wait." Our experience was just, "HURRY UP!" Production was like being shot out of a cannon. It also was the most fun part of the process. Once Jimmy called out, "Action!," we had arrived and decided to enjoy the ride. As prepared as we were, there were times when we simply had to improvise. Light was fading and our two-month-old cast member would not follow direction. But out of these and other "obstacles" ultimately came some of the best work.


### Postproduction

Once you finish production, you're halfway there. We found postproduction to be a combination of the technical and the creative. While both are incredibly educational, the creative parts were the most exciting to us: editing, sound design and mixing, working with musicians to create the score, looping lines with actors. Each step of post adds another layer to the film.

Every new artist who joined the project had his own idea of what he would like to bring to the overall vision; each had his own way of expressing a creative idea. Whether it was working with editors, musicians, illustrators, graphic artists, or sound designers, each had a unique way of communicating. At times, it felt like a language barrier. The challenge was to find a common ground and a way to collaborate.

For example, when scoring the film, there was a moment when suddenly the studio got silent. The instruments stopped, and the tension peaked. Everyone in the room was speaking a different language. Part of what got us through was trusting the musicians, and allowing "mistakes" on the way to finding what ultimately worked. If we recognized a sound that came close to what we had envisioned, we would work from there. Admittedly, sometimes we couldn't articulate what we wanted until we heard it.


### Distribution and Festivals

Each major city around the world has at least one major film festival. The opportunities to have our story seen far exceeded anything we'd ever experienced in theater. Eric's first film was *Cater-Waiter*. The film has screened as far away as Poland, Malta, and New Zealand. When a film really achieves its goal, it has the power to reach across cultures or languages and ultimately eliminate any barriers.

# Creating Your Own Theater Company

**T**he Group Theater was one of the most famous instances where actors (writers, directors) got together for a common cause— to make great theater. Over the decades, there have been many other famous American acting companies, all wanting to make their imprint. Aside from artistic reasons, some theater companies are created for political or social reasons.

### Banding Together with a Common Vision

There are several types of theater companies: the nonprofit companies, the commercial ones, and the actors' collectives (where actors pay a monthly fee).

Creating a theater company is a time-consuming and complex process. The group must write a mission statement stating why they've banded together, what their goals are, and what they hope to attain. Rules and goals must be set. Leaders and committees must be created to handle the day-to-day work.

Before the first show opens, there will be a great deal of preliminary work. It could take many months or even years before that first show. The potential play must be read and decided upon, money must be raised, a theater must be found, etc.

Being a member of a theater company is not for everyone. There is a great deal of tedious groundwork. But the idea of producing a successful company-generated show and being a member of an "artistic family" can be very rewarding.

### Theater Company Interviews

JOE STERN (**JS**) is the owner and artistic director of the Matrix Theatre, a Los Angeles theater company that has received the Drama Critics Circle Award for Best Production for an unprecedented four years in a row. A former actor, Stern and acting pal William Devane purchased the Matrix Theatre in the late 1970s. His productions have earned 150 theater awards, including 30 Los Angeles Drama Critics Circle Awards, 103 *Drama-Logue* Awards, 30 *L.A. Weekly* Awards, and 19 other awards from the L.A. Drama Critics Circle.

ROBERT LUPONE (**RL**) founded MCC Theater with co-artistic director Bernard Telsey in 1986, with a simple mission: to present new theatrical voices to New York audiences. For eighteen years, MCC Theater has accomplished this through three interrelated programs. A three-play season is committed to New York, American, and World Premieres, with plays such as Tim Blake Nelson's *The Grey Zone* (4 OBIE Awards), Margaret Edson's *W;t* (1999 Pulitzer Prize), Rebecca Gilman's *The Glory of Living* (2002 Pulitzer Prize finalist), and Neil LaBute's *The Mercy Seat* (published in *The Best Plays of 2002–3*).

SETH BARRISH (**SB**) is the co-artistic director of the Barrow Group, a company of actors, directors, playwrights, and designers. The company was founded in 1986. They co-produced the highly acclaimed production of *Old Wicked Songs*, which was nominated for the Pulitzer Prize. They received considerable attention for their productions of *Lonely Planet* by Steven Dietz (later co-produced Off-Broadway with the Circle Rep Company). The Barrow Group received a Drama Desk Award for Best Off-Off-Broadway Ensemble. They developed Martin Moran's *The Tricky Part* for a commercial run at the McGinn/Casale Theater in 2004.

**Whose idea was it to start this company? What were the reasons behind starting a new theater company? What were your goals?**

**JS**: Andrew Robinson, Larry Pressman, and Penny Fuller were three of the principal actors who started this company. The founding members also included Robin Gammel, Tony Giordano, Charles Hallahan, Mary Joan Nigro, and Cotter Smith. The Matrix Theatre has always existed. It was called Actors for Themselves. It did a couple of plays a year. We decided to move it into a different permutation in 1993 and call it the Matrix Theatre. Basically, the impetus was fiscal and artistic reasons. Simply, actors just can't afford to do theater anymore.

The idea was to double-cast every role. With understudies, the drop in skill level is tremendous. It always cheated the production and the audience. The idea was to maintain the quality of the productions. With double-casting all the actors, both casts would rehearse with the director at the same time. One actor would be in the audience and the other actor would be onstage. Then they'd alternate. It's as if the fictional character has two heads.

The reason for starting the company was to get a group of actors together to form a collective. The goal was simply to get actors to return to the theater, especially those who previously could not afford to do it. Another goal was to challenge both the actor and the audience. Each play we did had a different style. The American actor has become an endangered species because he can't afford to make a living anymore. And more and more are quitting the business after forty. The idea of the company was to be role models for younger actors, just like it was when I was younger. Younger actors working with older ones could learn as they worked. This country really doesn't support the arts. Artists will always create their own environment.

**RL**: I was teaching acting to eight students, and we all got bored after two years. We liked each other and wanted to stay together, so the next logical step was to form a theater company. The tradition was the Shakespearean actor-manager idea, where we'd read plays every week together and then try to formulate a theater. I was trying to find some theater roots for myself after working in this town for a number of years. I, personally, was in some ways confused. I followed along with Bernie's (Telsey) idea of starting a theater company, which was something he'd always wanted to do. Bernie, aside from being a theater major at NYU, was also a theater administration major. From 1983–86 we tried a for-profit company. We were going to work on new plays and then sell them at backers' auditions to producers. Then we'd go back to the studio and work on new plays. We did eventually get options for two Broadway plays. But the money wasn't enough to keep us afloat. Bernie convinced us that the best way to go on was to go nonprofit. For a while, we were at the Nat Horne Theater on Theater Row doing our one-acts, and then eventually, we got our own space.

**SB**: It was my and Nate Harvery's idea. It was a combination of factors. We were a group of actors looking for a place to be able to play and work in a way that was fun for us. We were young, just going out in the real world to work in various places. A lot of times, it was frustrating for different reasons. We had complaints about the directors we'd work with, the plays, whatever. We had become fascinated with an acting style that was particularly "documentary-esque," ultra-real. We didn't feel that we were expert at it, but it did interest us. Our main goal in acting was that the audience lose sight of the fact that they were watching an actor and feel like they were in a room with a real person. We didn't plan on producing, originally; it just worked out that way.

### What problems did you face originally? How did you eventually overcome them (if you did)?

**JS**: We didn't want this to be something competitive. When you have this double-casting, it can become that. We still have two opening nights, but in the beginning, the papers reviewed both nights. As the novelty wore off, there were fewer and fewer double reviews and more and more single reviews. Actors would be reviewed by the flip of a coin. So one actor would be reviewed, and the other not.

The way the company originated was that I invited eighty or ninety actors whom I had worked with over the years to a reading of a play. Afterward, we had a discussion about the play and whether we felt this system could work. I took the information from that meeting and then selected the first play. Another way we avoided competitiveness between actors was to cast two very different types for each role. In our first play, *The Tavern,* Cotter Smith and Robin Gammel played the same role. They are extremely different types. With this technique, we proved that there's more than one way to tell the truth. We'd have symposiums after each production with the actors, where we'd discuss what we could and couldn't improve. We discovered that this technique was most difficult on the directors. Directors had to carry the load. We started with four weeks of rehearsals and ended with six weeks. We started with two weeks of previews and then went to three weeks. We didn't want to shortchange the audience in terms of the critics and everything else. The great thing about Los Angeles theater is that because there's not really a contract, you have enough flexibility to expand the time to fit the work.

**RL**: Clarity—about what an artistic mission is, funding, overcoming ignorance (both artistically and financially), and working out the dynamic of relationships. An organization has many growth processes. You start off with enthusiasm and innocence, and then you work toward survival, and then, as you become more professional, volunteers fall by the wayside, so you have to hire a staff. It's all an evolution.

Bottom line: long hours, grit, and determination! How do you overcome the problems? With passion and belief in the theater. Always keeping in mind the importance and nobility of it.

**SB**: Raising money was the first major hurdle we came to. We were artists and we had to learn about the business side of the business. We hooked up with people who were adept at doing this type of work. A lot of it we just learned while doing, making horrible mistakes along the way, but always learning and getting better at it.

**What was your first public production? How did it go? What lessons did you learn from doing that production?**

**JS**: It was *The Tavern,* our biggest success. Tony Giordano, the director, had suggested the play. He had done it twice in the region. It was nominated for seven or eight L.A. Drama Critics Circle Awards, and it won for Best Play. It went incredibly well, was a huge hit. We learned that we needed more time to rehearse, that we needed most of the actors at all the rehearsals as much as possible. Especially at the beginning of the rehearsal of a play.

**RL**: It was the *Class One-Acts*, in 1986. We really didn't know what we were doing back then. One thing we learned was the amount of work it takes to put on a production. Also, the fragility necessary to corral all the creative talents, along with your own ignorance of any united vision.

**SB**: The first thing we did was a one-night event at the Perry Street Theater. We raised $7,000 that night. We did the public premiere of some of Joe Pintauro's plays. In some ways it went very well, in others, not. We put a ton of attention into the artistic side. We invited prospective board members. The evening was successful in that we got an instant board of directors. We were thrilled that we were able to pull it off. We learned about the process of working with each other and designers in a production mode. The main thing we learned was that it was possible to do.

### What are the advantages of being part of an artist-created theater company? Any disadvantages?

**JS**: The major thing is empowerment. It always has been. The actor has always been a third-class citizen up until the last fifteen years. He never directed or produced—he just acted. The actor has to be a producer to facilitate his own employment. That's been the major part of the explosion in L.A., with some 1,200 productions a year, mostly actor-driven. The main disadvantage is monetary. You don't get any grants. One thing to our advantage is that I own the building. The three years that I worked on *Law and Order*, I rented the building out and the money that I made was the seed money for the company. It's a nonprofit company.

**RL**: Shorthand and communication are a couple of the advantages. Working with other like minds toward a common vision is very rewarding, very satisfying. Some of the disadvantages are the diffi-culties you encounter in fund-raising, professional management of an office, marketing, getting an audience, advertising . . . The list goes on.

**SB**: The advantage is that you quickly learn that there are no excuses. You get a constant reality litmus test about how you're doing. It's easy to blame the world and not really grow. Also, you develop a working shorthand with people, so that certain kinds of things can happen quickly. There's a possibility for a kind of aesthetic that everybody shares. The disadvantage is, you attach yourself to a family that's bound to be dysfunctional. As people grow, their agendas change, and you sometimes have to compromise or separate.

**What advice do you have for other actors wanting to start their own company?**

**JS**: What I did was that I got all my friends, who I had worked with and trusted and had prior relationships with, together. These were all wonderful actors. I recommend other actors wanting to start their own company to do the same thing. Then you must eliminate those people with personal agendas. You must be able to depend on every person in your company. They must have character. There's very lit-tle money or contractual obligations so you must be certain that they're team players. You must all have a very like mind to collabo-rate. Intuitively, you must know who will be able to work well in such a close collaboration as a theater company.

There are two things that destroy all companies. A cancer from within because of bad behavior, bad character, and the inability to be part of a team; and, to a certain degree, expansion. Also, don't com-promise the art of what you're doing by allowing people who aren't gifted to enter the company by volunteerism.

**RL**: If you want to start a theater company so you can act, don't do it. If you want to start a theater company so you can say something about the world we live in, that's a good reason. Involving myself with this theater has taught me a lot about interpersonal relation-ships, and that has impacted on me as an actor. I've had to talk with press people, public relations people, even fellow employees. By and large, it's been immensely rewarding.

**SB**: Terence McNally's advice to me about creating my own theater company was, "Be patient. It's a long haul." Someone really has to be in charge. It makes things much easier. Originally, we started off as a democracy, but we learned that a group functions best with a leader.

# Artists' Support Organizations, Career Consultants, and Life, Career, and Creativity Coaches

**A**s most actors have learned, money is not an easy thing to come by as you are promoting and developing your acting career. Fortunately, there are organizations that assist actors, performance artists, and theater companies to lighten their loads.

### Helping You Help Yourself

Most of these organizations are not-for-profit groups that help performers with everything from getting grants to press coverage to rehearsal space to all sorts of technical assistance. I am listing just a few New York City–based organizations. There are many more all over the country.

**Dance Theater Workshop**
219 West 19th Street, New York, NY 10011
(212) 691–6500
*www.dtw.org*

Dance Theater Workshop (DTW) is a not-for-profit, community-based organization that provides artist sponsorship programs and production facilities as well as a broad spectrum of administrative, promotional, and technical services to the community of independent artists in New York and across the country. Such notable artists as Whoopi Goldberg, Bill Irwin, and Paul Zaloom (to name just a very few) found an early artistic home at Dance Theater Workshop. The workshop's mission is "to identify and nurture emerging and maturing contemporary artists working in diverse cultural contexts; to stimulate and develop a broader audience for these artists and their work; and to create opportunities within which these artists can create by providing an interactive community laboratory for the working imagination and its essential, practical application to the world that surrounds us."

Founded in 1965 by Jeff Duncan, Art Bauman, and Jack Moore, DTW is a multifaceted organization devoted to developing programs and resources that help independent artists grow professionally while increasing the public's involvement in the arts. Dance Theater Workshop is one of the country's most active producers of new talent.

Each member receives a membership kit that helps artists plan and execute performances. The kit helps the performer keep track of preproduction deadlines, schedules, and procedures, as well as more general administrative and technical needs. Members also receive a press reference kit, which includes updated press lists, information on what to include in a press release, and general specifications on what makes a useful press photograph. The kit even includes press label sets for your press release mailings, organized by publication deadline. DTW has a complete mailing preparation service (which includes labeling, bundling and sorting, bagging, and post office delivery) that enables performers to save on postage costs by using DTW's nonprofit bulk-mail permit.

Another service that Dance Theater Workshop provides is a low-cost video service that includes recording, postproduction, and viewing facilities.

DTW offers financial assistance for performers through different grants and funds.

## The Field

161 Sixth Avenue, New York, NY 10013
(212) 691–6969; fax (212) 255–2053
info@thefield.org
*www.thefield.org*

The Field offers programs that help independent artists create new artwork, manage their careers, and develop long-range strategies for sustaining a life in the arts. All of The Field's programs are non-curated and are open to artists who create original work in dance, music, performance art, text, and theater.

- **Art-Based Programs**. Fieldwork is a weekly peer-feedback workshop where artists can share developing work in a format designed by artists. Fielday is a non-curated opportunity for artists to develop their work through performance. Works can be shown in various stages of development.
- **Artward Bound** is a free group artist residency. It sends artists to rural retreat centers to make new work and focus on personal career development.
- **Career-Based Programs**. These programs include workshops such as "Grant Writing," "Management Nuts & Bolts," and "Ready to Book," which give artists and administrators the tools needed to develop and maintain their artistic careers.
- **Services**. The Non-Profit Sponsorship program provides independent performing artists and groups with eligibility to apply for most grants that require a 501(c)(3), not-for-profit status; to receive tax-deductible donations from individuals; to access Materials for the Arts and the Costume Collection; and for reduced rental rates for certain performance spaces.
- **IPARC**—Independent Performing Artists Resource Center. Located at The Field's office, IPARC offers fund-raising resources and hands-on assistance: databases such as the Foundation Directory Online, computer workstations, and a library of books, journals, and information directories. One-on-one assistance and consultations are also available to guide users through grant writing and other fund-raising endeavors.

- **GoTour**. GoTour (*www.gotour.org*) is a free Web site that gives independent artists the resources they need to take their show on the road. Visitors log on for free and access a national arts network where they can search for venues, network with artists nationwide, find media contacts, read advice from other artists and arts professionals, add information on their local arts community, post tour anecdotes, and list concert information and classified ads.
- **Field Forward Network**. Through the Field Forward Network, The Field's programs are offered in sixteen U.S. cities and Tokyo, Japan. The Network's mission is to create a community of independent performing artists and facilitate communication among the Network sites. Currently sites are located in Atlanta, Chicago, Houston, Miami, North Adams (MA), Philadelphia, Phoenix, Plainfield (MA), Raleigh (NC), Richmond (VA), Rochester (NY), Salt Lake City, San Francisco, Seattle, Tucson, Washington, D.C., and Tokyo, Japan.

## Franklin Furnace

112 Franklin Street, New York, NY 10013–2980
(212) 925–4671; fax (212) 925–0903
*www.franklinfurnace.org*

Martha Wilson founded Franklin Furnace twenty-five years ago as a place for avant-garde and performance artists to develop their projects.

According to its mission statement, "Franklin Furnace is dedicated to serving artists by providing both physical and virtual venues for the presentation of time-based visual art, including but not limited to artists' books and periodicals, installation art, performance art, and 'live art on the Internet'; and to undertake other activities related to these purposes. Franklin Furnace is committed to serving emerging artist and their ideas, and to assuming an aggressive pedagogical stance with regard to the value of avant-garde art to cultural life."

It offers these services to artists:

- Sequential Arts for Kids places professional artists in the New York City public school system.

- Franklin Furnace Fund for Performance Art presents performance art, both live and cybercast through the Internet.
- Fund for Performance Art, which is supported by the Jerome Foundation and the Joyce Mertz-Gilmore Foundation. Franklin Furnace awards grants of $2,000 to $5,000 to emerging artists, allowing them to produce their work anywhere in New York State.

### Acting Career Consultants

Career consultants help actors plan their future in show business. I've seen some very talented actors remain out of work simply because they didn't have a plan, a way to deal with the business aspects of show business. I discussed the role of the career consultant with Sue Henderson of Henderson Enterprises to learn of exactly how her company guides actors.

The career consultant helps the actor with all the necessary promotional tools and skills. She starts by talking to the actor to find out what "type" the actor is, and what areas of the business he wants to work in. Then she'll give him appropriate (for that actor) photographer suggestions. She'll provide the actor with resources for reproduction of photos and composites, and postcards and envelope providers. She'll consult with the actor regarding what type of eight-by-ten would be appropriate. In addition, the career consultant will help the client develop an effective cover letter and work with him on his resumes.

The career consultant finds out what kind of training the actor has already encountered; then she will help the actor plan future training based on his career needs and wishes. She will refer the actor to a variety of teachers, and advise him to audit classes or meet with teachers before beginning study.

She'll discuss the importance of contacting production companies and cable companies for work. There are production companies that use both union and non-union talent and have their own in-house casting. The consultant will help the actor select which production and cable companies might be interested in that particular actor.

When a client is artistically ready, the career consultant will suggest agents and managers to target. Networking and even grooming tips are dealt with.

The consultant will help to educate the actor (client) as to how the business works. She'll explain the *Ross Report*, breakdowns, and the differences between the NY and L.A. market. She'll let the actor know specifically what casting directors, agents, and managers look for and how to meet them. The consultant will target specific casting directors, agents, and managers for the actor and show him the necessary steps to take to meet with them. She'll also discuss the pros and cons of becoming a union actor, and let the actor know when she thinks it would be appropriate for him to join. She'll give him the tools to figure out which "free" endeavors, like showcases, will be worthwhile, and which ones will not help his career.

Along with discussing when and how clients are paid for different jobs, she'll explain the different commissions that are due to agents, managers, etc. She'll prepare the actor to face his accountant at tax time, explaining how to keep track of his personal finances in a businesslike manner.

### Life, Career, and Creativity Coaches

Sharon Good of Good Life Coaching (*www.goodlifecoaching.com*), a life, career, and creativity coach, says that a life coach works with actors to help them package themselves well, target the jobs they want, and follow through with consistent action. A life coach can help you develop focus and discipline in marketing yourself, as well as bolstering your confidence through discouragement of the self-doubt that actors are prey to.

Having a coach is like having a partner in your career. With a coach, you can be more organized and disciplined with your self-promotion, and having someone to report to will help motivate you to follow through. By providing objective feedback and support, a life coach can help you:

- Clarify your professional image and career objectives
- Present yourself professionally
- Plan your self-promotion strategy
- Take more consistent action
- Build and maintain confidence
- Maximize your time and resources
- Get more jobs

# New York Theaters

## Broadway Theaters

The Ambassador Theatre, 219 West 49th Street

The American Airlines Theatre, 227 West 42nd Street

The Broadhurst Theatre, 235 West 42nd Street

The Brooks Atkinson Theatre, 257 West 47th Street

The Ethel Barrymore Theatre, 243 West 47th Street

The Vivian Beaumont Theatre, 150 West 65th Street
(Lincoln Center)

The Belasco Theatre, 111 West 44th Street

The Biltmore Theatre (Manhattan Theatre Club),
263 West 47th Street

The Booth Theatre, 222 West 45th Street

The Broadhurst Theatre, 235 West 44th Street

The Broadway Theatre, 1601 Broadway (at 53rd Street)

Circle in the Square Theatre, 1633 Broadway (at 50th Street)

The Cort Theatre, 138 West 48th Street

Ford Center for the Performing Arts, 213 West 42nd Street

The Gershwin Theater, 222 West 51st Street

The John Golden Theatre, 252 West 45th Street

The Helen Hayes Theatre, 240 West 44th Street

The Hirchfeld Theatre, 302 West 45th Street

The Imperial Theatre, 249 West 45th Street

The Walter Kerr Theatre, 219 West 48th Street

The Longacre Theatre, 220 West 48th Street

The Lunt-Fontanne Theatre, 205 West 46th Street

The Lyceum Theatre, 149 West 45th Street

Thc Majestic Theatre, 247 West 44th Street

The Marquis Theatre, 1535 Broadway (at 46th Street)

The Minskoff Theatre, 200 West 45th Street

The Music Box Theatre, 239 West 46th Street

The Nederlander Theatre, 208 West 41st Street

The New Amsterdam Theatre, 212 West 42nd Street

The New Victory Theatre, 209 West 42nd Street

The Eugene O'Neil Theatre, 230 West 49th Street

The Palace Theatre, 1564 Broadway (at 47th Street)

The Plymouth Theatre, 236 West 45th Street

The Richard Rodgers Theatre, 226 West 46th Street

The Royale Theatre, 242 West 46th Street

The St James Theatre, 246 West 44th Street

The Shubert Theatre, 225 West 44th Street

The Neil Simon Theatre, 250 West 52nd Street

Studio 54, 254 West 54th Street

The Virginia Theater, 245 West 52nd Street

The Winter Garden Theater, 1634 Broadway (at 51st Street)

## Off-Broadway Theaters

### The Theater District
The Abington Theatre, 432 West 42nd Street

ATA, 314 West 54th Street

City Center Theatre, 131 West 51st Street
Creative Place Theatre, 750 Eighth Avenue
Douglas Fairbanks Theatre, 432 West 42nd Street
The Duke On 42nd Street, 229 West 42nd Street
Ensemble Studio Theatre (E.S.T.), 549 West 42nd Street
47th Street Theatre, 304 West 47th Street
Harold Clurman Theatre, 410 West 42nd Street
Intar (Hispanic American Arts Theatre), 508 West 53rd Street
Irish Arts Center, 553 West 51st Street
John Houseman Theatre, 450 West 42nd Street
John Jay Theatre, 899 Tenth Avenue
Jose Quintero Theatre, 534 West 42nd Street
Lambs Theatre, 130 West 44th Street
Lion Theatre, 410 West 42nd Street
Manhattan Theatre Club, 131 West 55th Street
Medicine Show Theater, 549 West 52nd Street
Mint Theater, 311 West 43rd Street
New Victory Theater, 209 West 42nd Street
Pantheon Theatre, 303 West 42nd Street
Pelican Studio/New Perspectives, 750 Eighth Avenue
Phil Bosakawski Theatre, 354 West 45th Street
Primary Stages, 354 West 45th Street (also at 59 East 59th Street)
Producers Club, 358 West 54th Street
Pulse Ensemble Theatre, 432 West 42nd Street
Samuel Beckett Theatre, 410 West 42nd Street
Second Stage Theatre, 307 West 42nd Street
Signature at Peter Norton Space, 555 West 42nd Street
Studio Theatre, 145 West 46th Street
Theater at St. Clement's, 423 West 46th Street
Theater Four, 424 West 45th Street
Theatre 3, 311 West 43rd Street
Town Hall, 123 West 43rd Street
Trilogy Theatre, 341 West 44th Street

Vital Theatre, 432 West 42nd Street

Westside Downstairs (and Upstairs) Theatre,
407 West 43rd Street

### The East Village and the Lower East Side

Astor Place Theatre, 434 Lafayette Street

Bleecker 45, 45 Bleecker Street

Bouwerie Lane Theatre, 330 Bowery

Classic Stage Company, 136 East 13th Street

Collective Unconscious Theatre, 145 Ludlow Street

Connelly Theatre, 220 East 4th Street

Clement Soto Velez Cultural Center, 107 Suffolk Theater

Elysium Theatre, 204 East 6th Street

Henry Street Settlement Theatre, 465 Grand Street

Jean Cocteau Repertory Theatre (at the
Bouwerie Lane Theater)

Kraine Theatre, 85 East 4th Street

La MaMa Theatre, 74A East 4th Street

Metropolitan Playhouse, 220 East 7th Street

New York Theatre Workshop, 79 East 4th Street

Orpheum Theatre, 126 Second Avenue

Pan Asian Repertory, 47 Great Jones Street

Pearl Theatre, 80 St. Marks Place

Present Company, 198 Stanton Street

Prometheus Theater, 239 East 5th Street

P.S. 122, 150 First Avenue

Public Theatre, 425 Lafayette Street

Red Room Theatre, 85 East 4th Street

St. Marks Theatre, 94 East 4th Street

Surf Reality Theatre, 172 Allen Street

Theatre For The New City, 155 First Avenue

### The Financial District

Shooting Star Theater, 40 Peck Slip

**The West Village, Soho, and Tribeca**

Access Theatre, 380 Broadway

Actor's Playhouse, 100 Seventh Avenue South

Bank Street Theatre, 155 Bank Street

Castillo Theatre, 580 Greenwich Street

Circle in the Square (Downtown) 159 Bleecker Street

Duplex, 61 Christopher Street

Flea Theatre, 41 White Street

Greenwich House Theater, 27 Barrow Street

Greenwich Street Theatre, 547 Greenwich Street

HERE Arts Center, 145 Avenue of the Americas

Jane Street Theatre, 113 Jane Street

Lucille Lortel Theatre, 121 Christopher Street

Manhattan Ensemble Theatre, 55 Mercer Street

Manhattan Theatre Source, 177 MacDougal Street

Minetta Lane Theatre, 18 Minetta Lane

Ohio Theatre, 66 Wooster Street

Performance Garage, 33 Wooster Street

Players Theatre, 115 MacDougall Street

Rattlestick Theatre, 224 Waverly Place

Soho Playhouse, 15 Vandam Street

Soho Repertory Theatre, 46 Walker Street

Synchronicity Space, 55 Mercer Street

13th Street Repertory, 50 West 13th Street

Tribeca Playhouse, 111 Reade Street

Wings Theatre, 154 Christopher Street

**The Chelsea, Union Square, Midtown, Gramercy, Garment District, and Hell's Kitchen Areas**

Actor's Playground, 412 Eighth Avenue

Actor's Theater Workshop, 154 West 28th Street

Altered Stages Theatre, 212 West 29th Street

Atlantic Theatre, 336 West 20th Street

Blue Heron Arts Center, 123 East 24th Street

Cap 21, 15 West 28th Street

Center Stage Theatre, 48 West 21st Street

Century Center Theater, 111 East 15th Street

Chelsea Playhouse, 125 West 22nd Street

Dixon Place Theatre, 309 East 26th Street

DR2, 103 East 15th Street

East 13th Street Theatre, 136 East 13th Street

14th Street Y, 344 East 14th Street

Gloria Maddox Theatre, 262 West 26th Street

Gramercy Arts Theatre, 138 East 27th Street

Gramercy Theatre, 127 East 23rd Street

Hudson Guild Theater, 441 West 26th Street

Irish Repertory Theatre, 132 West 22nd Street

Maverick Theatre, 307 West 26th Street

MCC Theatre, 120 West 28th Street

Native Aliens' Flatiron Playhouse, 119 West 23rd Street

Sanford Meisner Theatre, 164 Eleventh Avenue

St. Luke's Theatre, 308 West 46th Street

Theatre 22, 54 West 22nd Street

Theatreworks/USA, 151 West 26th Street

Union Square Theatre, 100 East 17th Street

Urban Stages Theatre, 259 West 30th Street

Variety Arts Theatre, 110 Third Avenue

Vineyard Theatre, 108 East 15th Street

Zipper Theatre, 336 West 37th Street

**The Upper West Side and Upper East Side**

Arclight Theatre, 152 West 71st Street

Delacorte Theater, West 89th Street and Central Park West

Home Grown Theater, 2628 Broadway

Mazur Theater, 555 East 90th Street

McGinn/Cazale Theater, 2162 Broadway

Mitzi Newhouse Theatre, 150 West 65th Street

Playhouse 91, 316 East 91st Street

Promenade Theatre, 2162 Broadway

St Bart's Playhouse, 109 East 50th Street

78th Street Theatre Lab, 236 West 78th Street

Theatre East, 211 East 60th Street

Theatre Ten Ten, 1010 Park Avenue

Triad Theatre, 158 West 72nd Street

Westside Repertory Theatre, 252 West 81st Street

York (Theatre at St. Peter's), 619 Lexington Avenue

**Harlem**

Apollo Theatre, 126th Street (Martin Luther King Blvd.)

National Black Theatre, 2031 Fifth Avenue

# About the Author

**G**LENN ALTERMAN is the author of *The Perfect Audition Monologue, Two Minutes and Under (Volumes 1, 2, and 3), Street Talk (Original Character Monologues for Actors), Uptown, The Job Book: One Hundred Acting Jobs for Actors, The Job Book 2: One Hundred Day Jobs for Actors, What To Give Your Agent For Christmas, Two-Minute Monologs, Creating Your Own Monologue,* and *An Actor's Guide: Making It in New York City.*

*Two Minutes and Under (Volumes 1 and 2), Street Talk, Uptown, Creating Your Own Monologue, Promoting Your Acting Career, One Hundred Acting Jobs For Actors, The Job Book 2, Two Minutes and Under,* and *An Actor's Guide: Making It in New York City* were all Featured Selections in the Doubleday Book Club (Fireside Theater and Stage and Screen Division). Most of his published works have gone on to multiple printings.

His book, *The Perfect Audition Monologue,* was recently honored by the National Arts Club in New York City.

His plays *Like Family* and *The Pecking Order* were recently optioned by Red Eye Films (with Alterman writing the screenplay).

His latest play, *Solace*, was produced Off-Broadway by Circle East Theater Company and presently has several European productions. *Solace* was recently optioned for European TV.

*Nobody's Flood* won the Bloomington National Playwriting Competition and was a finalist in the Key West Playwriting Competition.

*Coulda-Woulda-Shoulda* won the Three Genres Playwriting Competition twice, including publication of the play in two separate editions of the Prentice Hall college textbook, *Three Genres: The Writing of Poetry, Fiction, and Drama*, by Stephen Minot. It has received several New York productions.

He wrote the book for *Heartstrings: The National Tour* (commissioned by the Design Industries Foundation For AIDS), a thirty-five-city tour that starred Michelle Pfeiffer, Ron Silver, Christopher Reeve, Susan Sarandon, Marlo Thomas, and Sandy Duncan.

Other plays include *Kiss Me When It's Over* (commissioned by E. Weissman Productions), starring and directed by Andre DeShields; *Tourists of the Mindfield* (finalist in the L. Arnold Weissberger Playwriting Competition at New Dramatists); and *Street Talk/Uptown* (based on his monologue books), produced at the West Coast Ensemble.

*Goin' Round On Rock-Solid Ground, Unfamiliar Faces*, and *Words Unspoken* were all finalists at the Actor's Theater of Louisville. *Spilt Milk* received its premiere at the Beverly Hills Rep/Theater 40 in Los Angeles and was selected to participate in The Samuel French One-Act Festival. It's had over twenty productions, most recently with the Emerging Artists Theater Company in New York. *The Danger of Strangers* won an Honorable Mention in both the Deep South Writers Conference Competition and the Pittsburgh New Works Festival, and was also a finalist in the George R. Kernodle Contest. There have been over fifteen productions of *The Danger of Strangers*, including shows by Circle Rep Lab, the West Bank Downstairs Theater Bar (starring *The Sopranos'* James Gandolfini), and the Emerging Artists Theater Company's One-Act Marathon. It was performed most recently at the Vital Theater Company on Theater Row in New York.

His work has been performed at Primary Stages, Circle in the Square Downtown, the Turnip Festival, HERE, La MaMa, the Duplex, Playwrights Horizons, and several theaters on Theater Row in New York, as well as at many other theaters around the country.

He is one of the country's foremost monologue and audition coaches, having helped thousands of actors in their search (and preparation) of monologues, as well as creating their own material for solo shows.

Glenn has lectured and taught at such diverse places as the Edward Albee Theater Conference (Valdez, Alaska), Southampton College, Governors School For the Arts (Old Dominion University), the School For Film and Television, Western Connecticut State College, Star Map Acting School of Long Island, the Dramatists Guild, the Learning Annex, the Screen Actors Guild, the Seminar Center, and the Boston public school system, as well as at many acting schools all over the country.

In 1994, he created the Glenn Alterman Studio (*www. glennalterman.com*), and through its auspices has worked privately as a monologue and audition coach and at colleges, universities, and acting schools all around the country.

His latest book of original monologues, *Two Minutes and Under, Volume 3* (Smith and Kraus), will be on the bookshelves in early 2005.

He presently lives in New York City, where he is working on a new commissioned play, writing a new screenplay, coaching actors, giving seminars, and occasionally working in film and TV.

# Index

Academy and Breakdown
  Services, Ltd., 86
*The Academy Players
  Directory*
  description of, 85–86
  online, 86
accents, 12, 13
acting career consultants,
  58, 227–28
actor directories, 85
Actors Access, 86, 87
The Actors Connection,
  101–2, 107
Actors Equity Association,
  70, 111, 156, 191, 193,
  194, 195–96
AFTRA (American
  Federation of
  Television and Radio
  Artists), 70, 111
agents. *See* talent agent(s)
answering services and
  pagers, 48, 49
artist, support organiza-
  tions, 223–28
Atlas Talent, 115
audition(s)
  acting teachers
    regarding, 4
  casting directors
    regarding, 1, 8, 143–44,
    145, 156, 157, 158,
    160–63, 165, 166
  directors and producers
    on, 69
  independent film, 207
  landing, 70
  preparation for, 1, 8, 17, 71
  talent agents on, 122–23,
    125

*Back Stage*, 12, 19, 70
Bacon, Kevin, 187

Baldwin, Alec, 187
Barrish, Seth
  advice from, 222
  background of, 216
  on theater company, 218,
    219, 220, 221
Barron, Doug, 48
Barrow Group, 216
Bascom, Fran
  actor dos and don'ts for,
    144
  actor interest for, 142
  actor interviews by,
    144–45
  auditions for, 145
  background of, 140
  career tips from, 147
  on headshots, 141
  on office contact, 146
  on resumes, 141
  show attendance for, 143
Basinger, Kim, 115, 125
Basset Talent Management,
  129
Bauman Hiller and
  Associates, 115
Becker, Rob
  actor advice from, 203–4
  background of, 198
  on creative team for
    show, 202
  one-man piece show by,
    198, 199, 200, 201,
    203–4
behavior, 122–23
Berle, Milton, quote from,
  56
Bernard Telsey
  Casting, 148
Better Business Bureau, 3
Bohlen, Lee K., on actor
  "product" marketing,
  60–62

Bohr, Jimmy
  actor dos and don'ts for,
    143
  actor interest for, 142
  actor interviews by, 144
  auditions for, 145
  background of, 140
  career tips from, 146
  on headshots, 140
  on office contact, 146
  on resumes, 141
  show attendance for, 143
Broadway Web Design, 92
Bryant, Ben
  background of, 79
  videographer and video
    editor expectations
    from, 83
  videotapes (reels) editing
    mistakes from, 81–82
  videotapes (reels) prepa-
    ration from, 80–81
Bryggman, Larry, 187

Canizares, Mike
  background of, 38
  on eight-by-tens and
    postcards, 39
  photo reproduction studio
    selection from, 38
  on problems with photos,
    38–39
  on reproduction expecta-
    tion for actor, 39
casting director(s)
  actor contact information
    for, 48
  actor directories for, 85
  actor interviews by, 67,
    68–70, 144–45, 159–60
  on auditions, 1, 8,
    143–44, 145, 156, 157,
    158, 160–63, 165, 166

casting director(s) (*Continued*)
  at casting seminars, 102–6
  contact with, 99–100
  cover letter for, 52–53, 57
  directors regarding, 137
  headshots for, 17, 20, 25,
    36, 140–41, 149–50
  interviews of, 139–66
  job description of, 137–38
  Kayser, Karen, commer-
    cial, 62–63
  Klassel, Shannon, 56
  list of daytime, 138–39
  mailing campaigns to, 51
  networking with, 98, 101
  online casting opinion
    from, 90
  personal manager rela-
    tionships with, 133–34
  postcards for, 54–56, 57
  producers regarding, 137
  on resume, 42, 43, 46
  for talent agent inter-
    views, 65–66
  talent agents regarding,
    120
  on training, 141, 151,
    165, 166
  types of, 60, 138
  videotapes (reels) for,
    73–74
  voice-cover, 183
CDs, 117–19
Chwat, Sam, 12–13
classes. *See* school(s);
  teacher(s); training
Clurman, Harold, 5
coaches. *See* teacher(s)
Cohen, Arthur
  background of, 31
  booking session with, 37
  cosmetic tips from,
    34–35
  new headshots advice
    from, 35
  on photo session, 32,
    36, 37
  on photographer
    selection, 32
  on shoot preparation, 33
  studio session includes, 36
  wardrobe recommenda-
    tion by, 34
commercial(s)
  casting director on, 69
  define your type in, 62–63
Conrad, Charles, 3
cosmetics, 22, 34–35
cover letter(s)

example, 53–54
Hochhauser, Hal,
  regarding, 52
  information included
    in, 53
  mailing campaign, 51
  new actor, 47
  Telsey, Bernard,
    regarding, 154
Cyd LeVin and
  Associates, 129

daily breakdowns, 86,
  120–21
Dainard, Michael, 59–60
dance schools, 14
Dance Theater Workshop,
  200, 201, 202, 223–24
Dauk, Jinsey
  background of, 31
  booking session with, 37
  cosmetic tips from, 35
  new headshots advice
    from, 35
  on photo session, 32,
    36, 37
  on photographer
    selection, 32–33
  on shoot prep-aration, 33
  studio session includes, 36
  wardrobe recommenda-
    tions by, 34
daytime serials, 138–39,
  187–88
De Niro, Robert, 205
demo tapes, 181–83
director(s), 13, 17
  auditions for, 69
  on casting directors, 137
  contact with, 99
  on resumes, 46
Donald Case Castings, 56
dos and don'ts, 122–23,
  143–44, 156–57,
  158–59, 161
*Drama-Logue,* 19

festivals, 211
The Field, 225–26
Field, Sally, 62
film(s), independent
  actor-filmmakers
    regarding, 207–12
  auditions for, 207
  books for, 206
  creation of, 205–6
  Georgiades and Lane on,
    212–14
  stage actors plus for, 206–7
finance, 170

Frankel, Gene
  background of, 3
  career advice from, 7
  class format, 6
  class technique of, 5
  interviews/auditions by, 4
Franklin Furnace, 226–27
Frimark, Merle
  financial considerations
    from, 170
  on publicist selection,
    168–69, 170, 171
Full House Productions, 182

Gage, Martin
  on actor behavior, 122
  actor interviews by, 119
  background of, 115
  career advice from,
    124, 125
  daily breakdown process
    for, 120
  on headshots, resumes
    and videotapes (reels),
    117–18
  job description of, 116, 121
  on locating talent, 116
  promotion suggestions
    from, 123
  talent choice for, 124
Garcia, Risa Bramon
  actor dos and don'ts for,
    157
  actor interest for, 152–53
  actor interviews by, 159
  auditions for, 161
  background of, 147
  career tips from, 165
  on headshots, 149
  on office contact, 163
  on resumes, 150
  show attendance for, 155
Georgiades, Jimmy, 212–14
Glasser, Marilyn
  career advice from,
    134–35
  on client jobs, 132
  job description of,
    129–30
  promotion suggestions
    from, 134
  talent agent and casting
    director relationships
    for, 133
  talent consideration by,
    131
Gold, Lisa
  on casting seminars,
    103–6
  on talent tours, 107–10

Gold, Sid
  career advice from, 135
  on client jobs, 132
  job description of, 130
  promotion suggestions
    from, 134
  talent agent and casting
    director relationships
    for, 133
  talent consideration by,
    131
Golden, Peter
  actor dos and don'ts for,
    157, 161
  actor interest for, 153
  actor interviews by, 159
  auditions for, 161–62
  background of, 147
  career tips from, 165
  on headshots, 149
  on office contact, 163
  on resumes, 151
  show attendance for, 155
Goldstar Talent
  Management, 129
Good, Sharon, of Good Life
  Coaching, 228
Group Theater, 215

hair. See cosmetics
Harrelson, Woody, 115, 125
Hawks, Robert, 206–7
headshot(s). See also
  photographer(s)
  advice about new, 35–36
  casting directors
    regarding, 17, 20, 25,
    36, 140–41, 149–50
  color, 28
  hair and makeup,
    22, 34–35
  image created by, 17–18
  photo session, 23, 32, 36
  photographer selection
    for, 19–21, 32–33
  preparation for, 21–22,
    33–34
  promotional marketing
    companies for, 51,
    57–58
  reproductions of, 26, 28,
    38, 39
  resume with, 41
  retouching, 25–26, 38
  selection of, 19–20, 25
  talent agents regarding,
    117–19
  type of, 18, 23, 28
  on videotapes (reels),
    74, 75

vs. postcard for mailing
    campaigns, 54–55
  wardrobe for, 21–22, 34
Henderson, Sue, 58, 227–28
Hepburn, Katharine, 64
Hirschfeld, Marc
  actor dos and don'ts
    for, 157
  actor interest for, 153
  actor interviews by, 159
  auditions for, 162
  background of, 147
  career tips from, 165
  on headshots, 149
  on office contact, 164
  on resumes, 151
  show attendance for, 155
Hochhauser, Hal
  background of, 57
  on cover letter, 52
  on postcards, 54–55, 57
Holtzer, Glenn
  on agent response to
    demo tapes, 183
  background of, 179
  on demo tape creation,
    181, 182 183
  on demo tape length, 183
  promotion types
    from, 184
  on studio selection, 182
  on voice-over casting
    directors, 183
  on voice-over
    salaries, 184
  voice-over training
    advice from, 180
How to Market Yourself
  (Dainard), 59
Howard, Stewart
  actor dos and don'ts for,
    158
  actor interest for, 154
  actor interviews by, 160
  auditions for, 163
  background of, 148
  career tips from, 166
  on headshots, 150
  on office contact, 164
  on resumes, 151
  show attendance for, 156

image consultant, 63–64
Independent Consulting
  for Independents, 206
Internet
  casting companies on,
    89–90
  entertainment industry
    services on, 86–87

Franklin Furnace
  performances on, 226,
    227
National Conference of
  Personal Managers on,
    128
  photographer Web sites
    on, 19, 33
  pros and cons of, 90
  suggested Web sites on,
    90–92
  Web site creation on, 92
interview(s)
  of acting teacher, 3–8
  by casting director, 67,
    68–70, 144–45, 159–60
  of casting director,
    139–66
  definition of, 64
  improvisation for, 68–69
  independent actor-
    filmmaker, 207–12
  of one-person show,
    198–204
  of personal manager,
    129–35
  of photo reproduction
    studio owner, 37–40
  of photographer, 31–37
  preparation for, 68, 69–70
  of publicist, 168–71
  of talent agent, 115–25
  by talent agents, 65–66,
    68–70, 119
  of theater company
    owner, 216–22
  types of, 69–70
  of video editor, 79–84
  of voice-over specialist,
    179–84
Inzetta, Patrick
  as actor and director in
    film, 210
  on festivals, 211
  on postproduction,
    209–10
  preproduction for, 207,
    208, 209
  production advice from,
    211–12

Joanna
  background of, 80
  videographer and video
    editor expectations
    from, 83–84
  videotapes (reels) editing
    mistakes from, 82
  videotapes (reels)
    preparation from, 81

Johnson, Sally
  background of, 3
  career advice from, 7
  class format, 6
  class technique of, 5
  interviews/auditions
    by, 4

Kayser, Karen
  on commercial types,
    62–63
  online casting opinion
    from, 90
Kim, Robert
  background of, 31
  booking session with, 37
  cosmetic tips from, 35
  new headshots advice
    from, 35–36
  on photo session, 32,
    36, 37
  on photographer
    selection, 33
  on shoot preparation,
    33–34
  studio session includes,
    37
  wardrobe recommenda-
    tions by, 34
Klassel, Shannon, 56
Kline, Kevin, 187
Krauz, Laurie, 63–64
Kreindler, Scott E.
  career advice from, 135
  on client jobs, 133
  job description of, 130,
    132
  promotion suggestions
    by, 134
  talent agent and casting
    director relationships
    for, 133–34
  talent consideration by,
    131
Kulage, Kristine, 92

Lane, Eric, 212–14
Levine, Bunny, 101–2
Liebhart, Vince
  actor dos and don'ts for,
    143–44
  actor interest for, 142
  actor interviews by, 144
  auditions for, 145
  background of, 140
  career tips from, 146
  on headshots, 141
  on office contact, 146
  on resumes, 141
  show attendance for, 143

The Link, 86
Los Angeles
  casting director inter-
    views, 139–66
  color headshots in, 28
  list of daytime casting
    directors in, 139
  networking facilities in,
    101
  photographer interviews,
    31, 32, 33, 34, 35,
    36, 37
  resume, 42, 45–46
  talent agent interviews,
    115–25
  talent tours in, 107–10
  video editing in, 80
  videotapes (reels) in, 73
Lupone, Robert
  advice from, 221–22
  background of, 216
  on theater company,
    217–18, 219, 220–21

mailing campaign(s)
  Glasser, Marilyn,
    regarding, 134
  marketing aspects of,
    26–27, 51–58, 62, 203,
    211
  Neeley, Michael,
    regarding, 51–52
  postcard examples for,
    55–56
  postcard vs. headshot for,
    54–55
  production, 191
  promotional marketing
    companies for, 51,
    57–58, 224
  talent agent, mass, 67
makeup. See cosmetic tips
manager(s), personal
  contracts and commis-
    sions for, 128
  interviews, 129–35
  job description of,
    127–28, 129–30
  Purcell, on roles of,
    127–28
  warning about, 128
marketing
  actor "product," 60,
    61, 119
  buy/sell line of, 61
  cover letter for, 52–54
  Dainard, Michael,
    definition of, 59–60
  headshots for, 17, 18, 21,
    25, 28, 33, 39,

image consultant for,
    63–64
  Internet for, 89–92
  mailings for, 26–27,
    51–58, 62, 203, 211
  photo business cards for,
    28, 40
  postcards for, 27–28, 39,
    40, 54–56, 57, 76, 176
  promotional companies
    for, 51, 57–58, 224
  tool, 28, 166
  type definition for, 21,
    60, 61–63
  videotapes (reels) for, 27,
    63, 73–77
  voice-over demos for,
    181–83
Martin, Colin
  actor advice from, 204
  background of, 198–99
  on creative team for
    show, 202
  one-man piece show by,
    198, 199, 200–202, 203,
    204
Martin Gage Agency, 115
Matrix Theatre, 216, 217
MCC Theater, 216
McCorkle, Pat
  actor dos and don'ts for,
    158
  actor interest for, 154
  actor interviews by, 160
  auditions for, 163
  background of, 148
  career tips from, 166
  on headshots, 150
  on office contact, 164
  on resumes, 151
  show attendance for,
    155–56
McCorkle Casting, 148
Meisner, Sanford, 3
  technique of, 2, 6
Method, the, 2, 6
Monroe, Marilyn, 64
The Motion Picture,
    TV, and Theater
    Directory, 175

Natarno, Jan, 80
National Conference of
    Personal Managers, 128
Neeley, Michael
  as actor, writer and
    producer in film, 210
  on festivals, 211
  on mailing campaigns,
    51–52

on postproduction,
210–11
preproduction for, 207–8,
209
production advice
from, 212
networking, 7
career goals for, 94–95
contacts for, 94, 100
description of, 93–94
facilities, 66, 101–2
facility interviews, 103–6
follow-up, 99–100
Gage, Martin, regarding,
123
Glasser, Marilyn,
regarding, 134
locations for, 94
as marketing tool, 28, 166
skills for, 95–97
at social and business
events, 97–99
talent tours for, 107–10
New York
acting schools in, 8–12
acting teacher inter-
views, 3–8
artist support organiza-
tions in, 223–28
casting director inter-
views, 139–66
color headshots in, 28
dance schools in, 14
list of daytime casting
directors in, 138–39
networking facilities
in, 101
photographer interviews,
31–37
reproduction studio
owner interviews,
37–40
reproduction studios in, 26
resume, 42, 43–44
singing teachers/vocal
coaches in, 15
speech schools and
teachers in, 13–14
talent agent interviews,
115–25
talent tours in, 107–10
theaters in, 229–35
Nicholson, Jack, 62
Norton, Edward, 152
Nusbaum, Alan
background of, 58, 102
on casting seminars,
103–6
on talent tours, 107–10

O'Connor, Claire
on financial considera-
tions, 170
on publicist selection,
168–69, 170, 171
office contact, 99–100,
145–46, 163, 164, 165,
166
one-man piece show(s)
by Becker, 198, 199, 200,
201, 203–4
description of, 197–98
by Martin, 198, 199,
200–202, 203, 204
by Palminteri, 123, 205
by Zaloom, 198, 199, 200,
201, 203, 204
Openden, Lori
actor dos and don'ts for,
157
actor interest for, 153
actor interviews by, 159
auditions for, 161
background of, 147
career tips from, 165
on headshots, 149
on office contact, 163
on resumes, 150
show attendance
for, 155

Page, Geraldine, 115, 122,
166
Palminteri, Chazz,
one-man piece show
by, 123, 205
Pastorelli, Robert, 115, 123
Penn, Sean, 152, 156–57,
160
Perry, Frank, 156
Perry, Jonathan
background of, 79
videographer and video
editor expectations
from, 83
videotapes (reels) editing
mistakes from, 82
videotapes (reels) prepa-
ration from, 81
Peters, Bernadette, 115, 125
photographer(s). *See also*
headshot(s)
digital, 37, 39
headshot portfolio of,
20–21
on headshot selection,
19–20
interviews of, 31–37
publicity photos from, 46
on reproductions, 38

play(s)
actor, producer for,
190–92
booking theaters for,
193–94
budget for, 194–95
Equity code for, 195–96
one-person, 197–204
preproduction of, 192–93
reading, 192
scene showcases *vs.*,
187–90
union or nonunion, 195
Plaza Desk Top
Publishing, 48
*Production Screen Magazine*,
175
postcard(s)
casting directors
regarding, 145–46, 152,
163, 164
example, 55–56
as marketing tool, 27–28,
39, 40, 57, 76
on videotapes (reels), 76
postproduction, 209–11
Precision Photos, 29, 38
preproduction, 192–93,
207–8, 209
producer(s)
actors as, 189–96
auditions for, 69
on casting directors, 137
resume for, 46
production, 182, 191,
211–12
Professional Resumes, 48
promotion, 27, 51, 57–58,
63, 73–77, 123, 134,
184, 224
publicist(s)
interviews of, 168–71
job description of, 57–58,
167
Purcell, Gerard W., 127–28

Redanty, Mark
on actor behavior, 122–23
actor interviews by, 119
background of, 115
career advice from, 124,
125
daily breakdown process
for, 120
on headshots, resumes
and videotapes (reels),
118
job description of,
116, 121
on locating talent, 116–17

Redanty, Mark (*Continued*)
  promotion suggestions
    from, 123
  talent choice for, 124
Redford, Robert, 171
reproduction studio(s),
  photo
  New York, 26, 29, 33,
    37, 38
  owner interviews, 37–40
  postcards and headshots
    from, 27
Reproductions, 29, 33, 37
resume(s)
  Barron, Doug,
    regarding, 48
  body of, 43
  casting directors
    regarding, 141, 150–52
  content of, 2, 42
  directors on, 46
  heading of, 42, 43
  with headshots, 41
  for interview, 68
  Los Angeles, 45–46
  for new actors, 47
  New York, 43–44
  photo stills on, 46
  review excerpts on, 46–47
  services, 47–48
  talent agents regarding,
    117–19
  training on, 44, 45, 46
Rich, Shirley
  actor dos and don'ts for,
    156–57
  actor interest for, 152
  actor interviews by, 159
  auditions for, 160–61
  background of, 147
  career tips from, 165
  on headshots, 149
  on office contact, 163
  on resumes, 150
  show attendance for,
    154–55
Roberts, Julia, 159
Rosen, Charles
  actor dos and don'ts for,
    158–59
  actor interest for, 154
  actor interviews by, 160
  auditions for, 163
  background of, 148–49
  career tips from, 166
  on headshots, 150
  on office contact, 164
  on resumes, 152
  show attendance for, 156

*Ross Report*, 76, 175, 228
Ryan, Meg, 62, 159, 187

SAG (Screen Actors Guild),
  70, 111
The Sally Johnson Studio,
  3, 11
Sande Shurin Acting
  Studio, 3, 11
school(s). *See also*
  teacher(s); training
  dance, 14
  New York City acting,
    8–12
  selecting of, 2–3
  speech, 13–14
  voice-over, 184–85
seminar(s)
  about "How to Get Your
    Career Started," 116–17
  casting, 102
  protocol at casting, 103
Shakespeare Mailing
  Service, 48, 52, 54, 57
show attendance, 142–43,
  154–56
showcases, 187–96
Showfax, 86, 87
Shurin, Sande
  background of, 3
  career advice from, 7
  class format, 6
  class technique of, 5
  interviews/auditions by, 4
Smith, Susan
  on actor behavior, 123
  actor interviews by, 119
  background of, 115
  career advice from, 124,
    125
  daily breakdown process
    for, 120–21
  on headshots, resumes
    and videotapes (reels),
    118–19
  job description of, 116,
    122
  on locating talent, 117
  promotion suggestions
    from, 123
  talent choice for, 124
speech, 12–14, 145
*The Standard Directory of
  Advertising Agencies,* 175
Stanislavski, 6
Star Tracks, 182
Stern, Joe
  advice from, 221
  background of, 216

  on theater company, 217,
    218–20
  background of, 37
  on eight-by-tens and
    postcards, 39
Stewart, Cameron
  photo reproduction
    studio selection from,
    38
  on problems with photos,
    38
  on reproduction expecta-
    tion for actor, 39
Strasberg, Lee, 3, 5, 166
Stuart Howard Associates,
  148
studio sessions, photog-
  raphy, 36–37
Susan Smith and
  Associates, 115

talent
  choices, 124
  considerations, 131
  locations, 116–17
  tours, 107–10
talent agent(s)
  on auditions, 122–23, 125
  casting agents regarding,
    65–66
  on casting direct-ors, 120
  at casting seminars, 102,
    104
  CDs for, 117–19
  commissions of, 112
  as contact for casting
    directors, 163, 165, 166
  cover letter for, 52–53
  description of, 111
  freelance *vs.* signed, 112
  headshots for, 20, 25,
    117–19
  interviews by, 65–66,
    68–70, 119
  interviews of, 115–25
  mailing campaigns to,
    51, 56, 67
  marketing aspect of
    mailings for, 56
  networking facilities
    regarding, 66
  networking with, 98, 101
  personal manager rela-
    tionships with, 133–34
  postcards for, 54–56
  on resume, 46, 117–19
  seeking representation
    with, 67, 99–100, 112–13
  types of, 60

videotapes (reels) for, 73–74, 117–19
voice-over demo tapes for, 182–83
Wasser on, 112
teacher(s). *See also* school(s); training
interviews of New York, 3–8
selection of, 2, 12
speech, 12–14, 15
voice-over, 179, 180, 184–85
Telsey, Bernard
actor dos and don'ts for, 158
actor interest for, 153–54
actor interviews by, 160
auditions for, 162
background of, 148, 216, 217–18
career tips from, 166
on headshots, 150
on office contact, 164
on resumes, 151
show attendance for, 155
Templeton, Penny
Advanced On-Camera Class of, 7
background of, 4
career advice from, 7
class format, 6
class technique of, 6
interviews/auditions by, 4
Teschner, Mark
actor dos and don'ts for, 143
actor interest for, 142
actor interviews by, 144
auditions for, 145
background of, 139–40
career tips from, 146
on headshots, 140
on office contact, 145–46
on resumes, 141
show attendance for, 142–43
theater compan(ies)
creation of, 166, 215–16
New York, 229–35
owner interviews, 216–22
training. *See also* school(s); teacher(s)
for camera work, 3, 4, 5, 6, 7
casting directors regarding, 141, 151, 165, 166
on resume, 44, 45, 46

schools, 8–12, 13–15, 174, 184–85
techniques for, 1, 2, 3, 4, 5–6, 7, 8
voice-over, 174, 176, 177, 179–80
Turner, Kathleen, 187
TVI Actors Studio, 58, 102

**union** affiliations, 27, 42, 195, 228

*Variety,* 70
video editors, 79–84
videographers, 79–84
videotape(s) (reels)
for casting directors, 73–74
companies, 84, 224
content of, 74–75
in Los Angeles, 73
for new actors, 75–76
preparation, 81, 82
promotion of, 27, 63, 73–77
talent agents regarding, 117–19
targets to send, 76
tips for tracking, 76–77
Villar, Tracy, 153
*Voice-over Marketing Guide,* 175
voice-over(s)
career in, 173–74
casting directors, 183
demos, 181–83
description of, 173
myths and misconceptions about, 176–77
schools and coaches for, 174
specialist interviews, 179–84
studios, 181–82
tips for success in, 174
work, 175–76

**wardrobe,** 21–22, 34
Wasser, Jonn
on actor behavior, 122
actor interviews by, 119
on actors/talent agents, 112
background of, 115
career advice from, 124, 125
daily breakdown process for, 120

on headshots, resumes and videotapes (reels), 118
job description of, 116, 121
on locating talent, 116
promotion suggestions from, 123
talent choice for, 124
Weist–Barron, 12, 23, 179, 180
Willis, Bruce, 169, 171
Wilson, Martha, 226

**Y**eskel, Ronnie
actor dos and don'ts for, 157
actor interest for, 153
actor interviews by, 159
auditions for, 162
background of, 148
career tips from, 166
on headshots, 149
on office contact, 164
on resumes, 151
show attendance for, 155

**Z**aloom, Paul
actor advice from, 204
background of, 198
on creative team for show, 202
one-man piece show by, 198, 199, 200, 201, 203, 204
Zema, David
about myths and misconceptions of voice-overs, 176–77
on agent response to demo tapes, 182–83
on demo tape creation, 181, 182
on demo tape length, 183
promotion types from, 183–84
on studio selec-tion, 182
on voice-over casting directors, 183
voice-over description by, 173
*Voice-over Marketing Guide* by, 175
on voice-over salaries, 184
voice-over school, 185
voice-over tips from, 174
voice-over training advice from, 179–80

# Books from Allworth Press

Allworth Press is an imprint of Allworth Communications, Inc. Selected titles are listed below.

**An Actor's Guide: Making It in New York City**
*by Glenn Alterman* (paperback, 6 × 9, 288 pages, $19.95)

**Creating Your Own Monologue**
*by Glenn Alterman* (paperback, 6 × 9, 208 pages, $14.95)

**Acting that Matters**
*by Barry Pineo* (paperback, 5½ × 8½, 240 pages, $16.95)

**Improv for Actors**
*by Dan Diggles* (paperback, 6 × 9, 224 pages, $19.95)

**Mastering Shakespeare: An Acting Class in Seven Scenes**
*by Scott Kaiser* (paperback, 6 × 9, 256 pages, $19.95)

**Movement for Actors**
*edited by Nicole Potter* (paperback, 6 × 9, 288 pages, $19.95)

**Making It on Broadway: Actors' Tales of Climbing to the Top**
*by David Wienir and Jodie Langel* (paperback, 6 × 9, 288 pages, $19.95)

**Career Solutions for Creative People: How to Balance Artistic Goals with Career Security**
*by Dr. Ronda Ormont* (paperback, 6 × 9, 320 pages, $19.95)

**Technical Theater for Nontechnical People, Second Edition**
*by Drew Campbell* (paperback, 6 × 9, 288 pages, $19.95)

**The Art of Auditioning: Techniques for Television**
*by Rob Decina* (paperback, 6 × 9, 288 pages, $19.95)

Please write to request our free catalog. To order by credit card, call 1-800-491-2808 or send a check or money order to Allworth Press, 10 East 23rd Street, Suite 510, New York, NY 10010. Include $5 for shipping and handling for the first book ordered and $1 for each additional book. Ten dollars plus $1 for each additional book if ordering from Canada. New York State residents must add sales tax.

To see our complete catalog on the World Wide Web, or to order online, you can find us at *www.allworth.com*.